The Dharma of Unfaithful Wives and Faithful Jackals

ALSO BY WENDY DONIGER IN SPEAKING TIGER

The Hindus: An Alternative History

Reading the Kamasutra: The Mare's Trap and Other Essays on Vatsyayana's Masterpiece

The Ring of Truth: Myths of Sex and Jewelry

Beyond Dharma: Dissent in the Ancient Indian Sciences of Sex And Politics

Winged Stallions and Wicked Mares: Horses in Indian Myth and History

The Dream Narrative: The Dreams of God and Mortals in Classical Hinduism

An American Girl in India: Letters and Recollections, 1963–64

After the War: The Last Books of the Mahabharata

Women, Androgynes and Other Mythical Beasts

Dreams, Illusion and Other Realities

The Dharma *of* Unfaithful Wives *and* Faithful Jackals

Some Moral Tales from the *Mahabharata*

WENDY DONIGER

SPEAKING
TIGER

SPEAKING TIGER BOOKS LLP
125A, Ground Floor, Shahpur Jat, near Asiad Village,
New Delhi 110049

First published by Speaking Tiger Books in 2024

ISBN: 978-93-5447-541-2
eISBN: 978-93-5447-935-9

10 9 8 7 6 5 4 3 2 1

Typeset in Garamond Premier Pro by SŪRYA, New Delhi

Printed at Chaman Enterprises, New Delhi

This is a work of fiction. Names, places and incidents are either the product of the author's imagination or used fictitiously. Any resemblance to actual persons, living or dead, is entirely coincidental.

CONTENTS

V. Stories about Kings

VI. Stories about Indra, King of the Gods

VII. Stories about Shiva

Introduction

How did the tiger's mother dissuade him from killing the pious jackal? How did the mouse escape from the cat, the owl, the mongoose, and the hunter? Why did the sage turn his dog into a leopard, and then back into a dog? How and why did the old guru's young disciple enter the body of the guru's young wife, in his attempt to control and protect her? These and many other pressing questions are posed and answered in the thirty-six stories I am going to retell in this book.

They all come from the *Mahabharata*, a Sanskrit text of over 75,000 verses, composed in ancient India over many centuries, particularly between 300 BCE and 300 CE. It is divided into eighteen books, of which the first eleven tell the story of a great royal family, the Bharatas, that wages a devastating internecine battle known as the Great Bharata War. The twelfth and thirteenth books, the *Shanti* ('Peace') and *Anushasana* ('Instruction') *Parvans*, are largely dedicated to an *extremely* long discourse on dharma (religion, morality, social duty, the way things ought to be) that the old king, Bhishma, dying, delivers in response to questions from the reigning king, Yudhishthira.[1] I will include these introductory question-and-answer discussions as italicized preludes to my translation of the stories themselves.

In addition to its concern for dharma, the *Mahabharata*

also serves as a practical textbook for kings, and so is equally concerned about *artha*, political and material success. And as a book about men and women, it is also interested in *kama*, pleasure (including, but not limited to, sexual pleasure). These three form a triad, called 'the goals of a man's life' or 'the triple path', the creation of which is described by one of our texts (#25, 'How the Golden Age Disappeared, and the Sages Created the First King'). Some texts added a fourth goal, *moksha*, freedom from rebirth, about which the *Mahabharata* is also concerned; it boasts, in its final verses: 'Whatever there is here about dharma, politics, pleasure, and freedom, that is also found elsewhere; but what is not here is nowhere.' (18.5.38; all such numerical citations without textual attribution are from the critical edition of the *Mahabharata*.) But the *Mahabharata* usually speaks of just three goals, and regards *moksha* as something that may or may not happen at the end of a life on earth.

The incidental stories in the twelfth and thirteenth books of the *Mahabharata* are about all four human goals, but mostly about dharma. As a mythologist with a personal penchant for *adharma* (the absence or violation of dharma), I have always been concerned with rule-breakers, with the cracks in the surface of things, as against preachment and smooth moralizing. And so, in the past, I have ignored this section of the great text, writing instead about the final books (Sixteen, Seventeen and Eighteen), in which the heroes ultimately die and reach heaven and are reconciled with their enemies.[2]

But embedded in the often mind-numbing ethical discourse of Books Twelve and Thirteen are a number of good stories that are frequently very funny and occasionally quite weird. And these stories don't simply illustrate a moral lesson; the characters have a complex interiority. When Yudhishthira asks Bhishma a particularly tricky ethical or political question, he often replies, 'Actually, there is an old story about this very point...' and tells the story. Apparently, someone had the very good idea of leavening all that ponderous moralizing with stories, somewhat like the parables in the New Testament, which are often so much more memorable than the moral teachings. These Indian stories, however, are generally a good deal quirkier than the Biblical parables, as well as more imaginative and often far more complex. The characters in them are more conflicted and the plots have more twists. For this book, I have lifted the stories out of the moral diatribes in which they are embedded, rather like picking the plums out of a plum pudding.

Though primarily about kings, these stories are necessarily peopled by members of all four classes of ancient Indian society (on which the far more detailed caste system is overlaid): Brahmin (priest), Kshatriya (royal warrior), Vaishya (merchant or farmer), and Shudra (servant). We also encounter, from time to time, people ranked outside of and below even the lowest of the four Hindu classes, such as the outcaste (now called Dalit) hunters known as Chandalas, Nishadas or Shvapakas ('Dog-cookers').

Often the text offers a highly original variant of a familiar tale. Some of these are retellings of the great foundational myths of India, stories about the creation of death and the origin of human evil. Other stories are spirited and even satirical versions of the more usual flattering or ingratiating narratives about great kings, and still others deal with more mundane concerns such as families and men and women and our relationship with animals. These retellings often remind me of the revisionist recitals of the Greek myths in the film *Never On Sunday* (1960, directed by Jules Dassin), stories told by a woman in twentieth-century Athens (played by Merlina Mercouri) who, at the end of each traditionally tragic story, assures us that no one dies and 'everyone goes to the seashore'. In a similar way, stories of men and women, fathers and sons, kings and holy men, dogs and tigers, are often retold in these books of the *Mahabharata* with strange twists that make the grand visions very human and the gemlike anecdotes sharply meaningful.

A number of these stories involve *tapas*, which is not 'asceticism', as it is often translated, implying just going without food and sex. It is a kind of superhuman power produced indeed by fasting and chastity but also by spectacularly stringent physical practices as well as by closing down all the openings of the body. Often it takes the form of heat trapped when those openings are closed. The person who amasses *tapas* gains magical powers, particularly the ability to use the suppressed heat of the body in a number of useful ways, such as burning an enemy to death or, on the other hand, begetting a child. I have translated the noun/adjective *tapasvin*, 'one who has *tapas*', as 'man of *tapas*' (or 'woman of *tapas*', *tapasvini*), a rather rough and ungainly English equivalent but a better approximation than the usual translation, 'ascetic'. Closely related to *tapas* is yoga, which is neither a meditation nor a way to perfect your abs, but a technique that gathers together a person's physical and mental forces to produce powers similar to those of *tapas*. A person who has mastered *tapas* and yoga can perform spectacular feats, overpowering even some of the gods, especially those who are vulnerable through their lack of self-control.

Many of the stories in the *Shanti* and *Anushasana Parvans* are about wicked women; a few are about good women; and some of the stories about women are variants of better-known stories that were originally not about women at all. In addition, some of the stories about animals are really about women, some indeed about good women, such as the wise mother of the gullible tiger (#16). But the overwhelming majority of these tales are grotesquely misogynist stories about the wickedness, or at the very least the frailty, of women:

How Vipula Entered Ruchi to Control Her (#2)
How Bhangashvana Became a Woman (#3)
How Satyavati's Mother Corrupted Her Daughter's Pregnancy (#4)
How Ashtavakra Resisted Seduction by an Old Woman (#5)
How Ahalya Sent Uttanka to the Underworld to Get Earrings (#6)

And some, though fewer, are about women who, if not actively good, are at least not spectacularly evil:

How the Procrastinator Saved Gautama from Killing his Wife (#7)
How Sudarshana, the Son of Fire, Let His Wife Oghavati Sleep with Dharma (#8)
How Jamadagni Protected his Wife Renuka from the Sun (#9)
How Utathya Got his Wife Back from Varuna (#10)
How Durvasas Tormented and Rewarded Krishna and Rukmini (#11)
How Narada married King Srinjaya's Daughter (#12)

A lurid and notorious passage in this general section of the *Mahabharata* suggests violent punishments for both men and women who have committed sexual transgressions; among these sinners, the young student who sleeps with his old guru's young wife—literally, uses his guru's bed—is often a particular concern in these stories:

> The wicked man who sleeps with his guru's wife is to be killed by having him embrace a red-hot hollow metal column. Or he may cut off his own penis and his testicles and hold them in his cupped hands and walk southwest until he drops dead... When a woman transgresses, especially when she has already been restrained, she must carry out the same punishment as for men

> who violate the wives of other men. When she leaves the bed of a better man for a worse man, the king should have her eaten by dogs in a crowded public place.[3] Or the king should have the adulterous man bound on an iron bed that has been heated up, and the man is burnt there. The same punishment is prescribed for women who betray their husbands. (12.159.46–60)

A few centuries later, these ideas became the equivalent of canon law in the dharma text attributed to Manu:

> No man is able to guard women entirely by force, but a man can guard his wife entirely by using these means: he should keep her busy amassing and spending money, engaging in purification, attending to her duty, cooking food, and looking after the furniture. Good looks do not matter to them, nor do they care about youth; 'A man!' they say, and enjoy sex with him, whether he is good-looking or ugly. By running after men like whores, by their fickle minds, and by their natural lack of affection, these women are unfaithful to their husbands even when they are zealously guarded. The bed and the seat, jewellery, lust, anger, crookedness, a malicious nature, and bad conduct are what Manu assigned to women.[4]

In the stories that we are about to consider, it is the women who are primarily blamed for the sexual problems of both sexes.

I would give a great deal to know the marital history of the men who composed these texts, and also to know where they first heard the stories. Surely not from their mothers or their nurses? In the ancient Indian equivalent of a locker room? But perhaps it would be more useful to consider not the source but the legacy of this misogynist mindset, in the dharma texts' insistence on the strict control of women and, ultimately, in the widespread and unpunished violence towards women in present-day India.

On the other hand, some of these stories have nothing but

good things to say not only about women who *do* fulfil their (strictly dictated) roles as wives and mothers, but also about a few independent women who, like good men, lead highly moral lives and achieve great *tapas*. For the spectacular misogyny of the *Mahabharata* is occasionally matched by phylogyny, the love of women, both individual women and certain types of women, primarily mothers. Even the wildly misogynist Bhishma admits that there are *some* good women: 'All women, always, are of two sorts, good and evil. The good women are fortunate, honoured, the mothers of the world, and they uphold this earth, with its forests and groves. The ones who are not good have evil intentions; they behave badly and destroy their families. They can be recognized by the evil marks that arise spontaneously on their limbs.' (13.41)

The stories about fathers and sons, that follow upon the heels of the stories of men and women, clearly rest upon this assumed base of ideas about gender and the nuclear family, but so, perhaps less explicitly, do the stories about animals, about kings, about the origin of evil, and finally about the great gods Indra and Shiva. Each corpus builds upon an ancient shared base of fundamental ideas about dharma and the violation of dharma, intricately connected with the concepts underlying the body of *Mahabharata* mythology as a whole.

I. Stories about Women

The largely negative attitude towards women expressed throughout the *Mahabharata* is immediately apparent right at the start of a conversation that Bhishma reports when Yudhishthira says, 'I want to hear about the true nature of women, for women are light-minded and the root of all evils.' And Bhishma replies, 'They tell this ancient story about that, a conversation between the divine sage Narada and the whore Panchachuda.' In this passage, Narada first refers to Panchachuda as a whore (*pumschali*, literally 'one who runs after men') and then, in the very next line, he notes that she is a blameless Apsaras (a kind of heavenly courtesan, a celestial dancing girl, the traditional partner of the celestial musicians called Gandharvas). Panchachuda therefore speaks with ambivalent but supreme authority, and her condemnation of women is straight from the mare's mouth. Much of what she says was repeated in later Sanskrit misogynist texts, such as the text of Manu cited above.

When Narada asks Panchachuda to tell him 'the true nature of women', at first she protests, insisting that, 'Being a woman, I cannot blame women. You should not ask me to answer such a question. You yourself know what sort of creatures women are by nature.' But when Narada argues, 'Just tell the truth. There would be a fault in telling a lie, but no fault in telling the truth,' she makes up her mind, smiles sweetly, and begins to describe 'the eternal faults of women':

> Not even beautiful married women, born of good family, remain within the moral boundaries: that is the flaw in women. There

is nothing more evil than women, who are the root of all evil. Women are not satisfied with husbands who are famous, rich, handsome, and in the power of their wives; they will still resort to another man. Lacking any good dharma and abandoning all shame, we women enjoy the most evil men. A man who seeks a woman and gets close to her and serves her in small ways—*that* is the man that women desire. Not regarding the moral bounds as bounds, women remain with their husbands only because no men are trying to get them or because they are afraid of their relatives.

There is no man that they will not go to, nor do they attach any importance to age. Handsome or ugly, 'It's a man!' and they go to bed with him. Not fear, nor compassion, never money, nor relatives, lineage, or connections—nothing makes women stay with their husbands. Women of good family envy women who are young and independent and wear gorgeous jewellery and clothing. Even women who are beloved and constantly honoured and protected and controlled cling to hunchbacks, blind men, mutes and dwarves, to cripples and other despised men. If there is no way at all of getting to men, women will pervert one another rather than stay with their husbands. But only because they cannot get men, or because they fear their relatives, or because they fear being imprisoned or killed, do women stay alone.

Women are fickle by nature, hard to please, and as difficult to understand as the words of a wise man are for ordinary people. Fire is never sated by wood, nor the ocean by rivers, nor death by all the creatures, nor beautiful women by men. And here is another secret about all women: as soon as a woman sees an attractive man, her vagina gets wet. Women cannot even bear a superb husband who gives them all that they desire, who honours and conciliates and protects them. They do not care for an abundance of luxuries, or for piles of jewellery and money, as much as for the pleasures of sex. Death, destruction,

> hell, the subterranean fire in the mouth of the mare,[5] the blade of a knife, poison, a serpent, fire—women are all of these in one. (13.38.1–29)

The stories that follow in the first part of this section assume that women simply *are* like this and suggest ways that men might try to deal with them.

And yet, despite the various assertions in the texts that we shall consider, insisting that *all* women are evil, some texts actually do tell of women who were good mothers, or good daughters, or even, occasionally, good wives. Most of the time, their virtue is merely negative—they do *not* commit the sins that women are generally accused of in this text. But some of them (such as the tiger's mother, #16 in the third section of this book) display a wisdom superior to that of the men with whom they interact, and others (like the wife of Sudarshana, the son of Fire), go to extraordinary and very painful lengths to fulfil their dharma as good wives.

A. Bad Women

1. How Brahma Made Women Evil to Delude Men

At the very end of her diatribe, Panchachuda says, 'When the creator made the five great elements, and arranged the worlds, and made men and wanton women, right then the flaws were already there in wanton women.' (13.38.30) When Yudhishthira asks about women, Bhishma answers him by telling him this story that Panchachuda had alluded to, about the creation of women. Presumably, there were no women at all in the first creation, and that is why the original (male) creatures were still virtuous. But since, once they were created, women were given an evil dharma, they are just fulfilling their dharma when they seduce and destroy men. Therefore (it seems to me), they really ought not to be blamed for such behaviour. In any case, it is the duty of men to protect themselves.

When Bhishma declares, at the end, that women are 'always unsubdued', he implies that they remain untamed, like wild animals. Bhishma's story—framed before and after by more diatribes against women—expresses an ideology of which the key is the cluster of implications of the verb *raksh*, that we will see frequently applied to women in the stories we will consider: *raksh* means to control and to protect and to guard.

The Text

Yudhishthira said: 'Men here in the world are extremely attached to women, and so are women attached to men. But how do men become attached to women? And how do women become attracted to men or, on the other hand, repelled by them? And then, how is it possible for a man to control attractive women? You must tell me this. For these women deceive men with their power of illusion, and no man who has fallen into their hands can get free of them; they are like cows that seize upon new grass, and newer and newer grass. They laugh loudly with a man who laughs; they weep loudly with a man who weeps; they accept even an unpleasant man if his words are pleasant. Neither the cunning text that Brihaspati, the consigliere of the gods, knows, nor the one that Shukra, the consigliere of the demons,[6] *knows, surpasses what women know; I think Brihaspati and the others made the political textbooks by extracting the essence of the intelligence of women. And so, how can men control and protect women? Women say that what is true is false, and what is false is true. Since they are like this, how then can men here control them? This is my great doubt. Tell me! If they can be controlled in any way, if it is possible to do or has been done in the past, you ought to tell me!'*

Bhishma said:

There is no falsehood at all in what I have told you about women. On this subject I will tell you an ancient story about how, in the past, Vipula controlled and protected his guru's wife. But first let me tell you how Brahma created alluring women, and for what purpose. For there is nothing at all more evil than women. An alluring woman is a blazing fire, and the very power of Illusion.

We have heard that these creatures once obeyed dharma, and by themselves they became gods. But that worried the gods, who went to Brahma to tell him what was on their minds. As they stood, heads down, in silence, Brahma knew what the gods were thinking, and so he created women as sorceresses to delude men. In the earlier creation, women here were virtuous, but from that creation by Brahma they were born as sorceresses, devoid of virtue. For Brahma gave them desires, and the alluring women, greedy for what they desired, stirred up the men. Brahma then created anger as the ally of desire, and all the creatures fell into the power of desire and anger.

Women have no ritual at all: this is the dharma that was laid out for them. And since women have no sense nor any prayers, they are false: this is what the sacred texts say. Beds, couches, ornaments, food, drink, ignoble behaviour, bad speech and sexual pleasure—that's what the Creator gave to women. It is not possible for anyone to control them in any way, not even the Creator; and so how could it be done by men here on earth? By words, death, imprisonment, or various forms of torture—it is not possible to control women, for they are always unsubdued. [13.39–40]

2. How Vipula Entered Ruchi to Control Her

Before telling his story of the creation of women, Bhishma briefly remarked to Yudhishthira, 'But I did hear this in the past, about how, long ago, Vipula controlled and protected his guru's wife.' (13.40.2) After relating the myth of the creation of evil women we have just considered, Bhishma returns to the story of Vipula, a man who enters the body of a woman, Ruchi, to control and protect her.

This story incorporates another incident that occurs elsewhere in the *Mahabharata*, where it is not about women at all. The tale of Vipula and Ruchi involves a weird variant on a famous passage in the fifteenth book of the *Mahabharata* (the *Ashrama Parvan*,

'The Book of the Hermitage'), in which the sage Vidura, dying, leaves his dead body (from which his soul and his consciousness escape at his death) but projects his breath and his senses into the body of his brother, King Yudhishthira. Here is that passage:

> Vidura, deep in meditation, looked right at the king without blinking, yoking his own gaze to the other's gaze. The wise Vidura entered limbs with limbs, placing breaths in breaths, senses in senses. Using the power of yoga, Vidura entered the king's body. And then the king saw the body of Vidura just standing right there, its eyes fixed, emptied of consciousness.[7] (15.33.21–27)

In that story, the gifted male trespasser uses yoga to project his breath and senses into his brother's male body.

The very different story that we are about to consider borrows this idea of entering another body, but now the male trespasser transfers not merely his breaths and senses but his entire consciousness, and transfers it into a *female* body, making it a tale that we might suspect of carrying a sexual overtone. And indeed, it is a story about sex, a story that turns upon the cluster of implications of the verb *raksh*, which we have already seen applied to women, with its meanings of to control and to protect and to guard. We therefore begin with an unstated lexical assumption that the only way you can protect a woman (from men) is to control her—and the story tells us that you can't control her. The point of this story is therefore that it is *impossible* to keep wives from committing adultery—unless you have magic powers, particularly yogic powers. The story could also stand as a kind of satire on the much broader Indian genre of the eternal triangle, in which a very old and very chaste sage marries a gorgeous young wife and engages a handsome young disciple, with predictable results.

In this story, a man of *tapas*, Vipula, protects a woman, Ruchi, from being seduced by a notorious womanizer: Indra, king of the gods, lord of rain and lightning. The story of Indra's paradigmatic seduction of Gautama's wife, Ahalya, is alluded to briefly in this text, but her story is told at length in the *Ramayana*[8] and briefly elsewhere in this part of the *Mahabharata*, where (after the primeval adultery) Gautama is said to have castrated Indra and replaced his testicles with those of a goat or to have branded him with a thousand vaginas (12.329.1 and .14[9]) (an episode alluded to in this story of Vipula and Ruchi). Other versions of the story tell of Indra's embarrassment when all the vaginas begin to menstruate, or his relief when the thousand vaginas are transformed into the thousand eyes for which Indra has always been famous: as a king, he has a thousand spies; as a sky-god, a thousand stars.

The turning point comes when Vipula projects his voice out of Ruchi's body. For Ruchi still has her own consciousness, and wishes to speak, but Vipula overrides her impulse and projects from her mouth his voice, not hers. (We might seek an analogy in the situation of a student driver whose control of the car can be taken over at will by the driving instructor in the passenger seat.) That gives away the game, for Vipula speaks in Sanskrit, the religious and literary language which women in ancient India were not supposed to speak (they would speak in the vernacular), and the god Indra, hearing Sanskrit come out of a woman's mouth, knows that something fishy is going on. Indra is too powerful for any mortal—even a man of great *tapas* like Vipula—to challenge directly; yet Indra's notorious moral weakness (especially for other men's wives) makes him vulnerable to a man who has powerful *tapas*. And so, once Indra realizes how great Vipula's powers are, he retreats rather than engage directly with him.

Several centuries after the *Mahabharata*, a Sanskrit farce depicts a man who doesn't enter a woman's body while she is still inhabiting it but exchanges bodies with her. In that variant of the theme, a magician puts the soul of a courtesan into the body of a wandering mendicant, and vice versa. And the poet comments: 'The life's breaths of the woman, placed in the body of this Brahmin, will cause a transformation of his essence and his behaviour.'[10] In the resulting confusion, the courtesan thinks and acts like a yogi, and vice versa. Here gender clearly remains distinct from the invaded body: the Brahmin's body, filled with the courtesan's life's breaths, thinks and behaves like a courtesan, not like a Brahmin. It is certainly possible that this text was inspired by the much earlier story of Ruchi and Vipula. Buddhist mythology, too, teaches that, to become a Bodhisattva, a woman must have not only the body but the mind of a man. It is a rich theme.

Bhishma begins his story with yet another iteration of the boilerplate damnation of women.

The Text

Bhishma said: 'There is nothing at all false in what I am telling you about women. And on this subject, let me tell you an ancient history about how, in the past, Vipula controlled and protected a woman.

'The great sage Markandeya told this story to me long ago, one day on the banks of the Ganges. This is how it is possible for men to protect and control women—or else they cannot be protected and controlled. Women are sharp, and nothing is dearer to them than sexual union with men. They can be seduced or bought or acquired, but they do not take pleasure in just one single man. Men should have no affection for them, nor jealousy; women should be enjoyed only as a last resort, or for the sake of dharma. Otherwise,

a man would be destroyed. In all things, and everywhere, cunning is needed.

'Vipula protected a woman in this one single way; in this world of men, there is no other way to protect and control women.'

There was a famous sage named Devasharman. His wife, who was called Ruchi, was unparalleled on earth for her beauty. The gods and Gandharvas and demons were all intoxicated by her beauty, but especially Indra. Devasharman knew about the behaviour of women, and he controlled and protected his wife to the best of his powers and with his greatest efforts. He knew that Indra indulged his desires for other men's wives, and so he made a great effort to control and protect his wife. One day he decided to perform a sacrifice, but he worried, 'How can I protect my wife?' He thought of a means of protecting her; he summoned his beloved pupil Vipula and said, 'I am going to go away and perform a sacrifice, but Indra is constantly trying to get my wife Ruchi. My son, guard her as best you can. You must never get careless about Indra, for he can take on various forms.'

Now, Vipula had controlled his senses and was always fierce in his *tapas*. He knew dharma and spoke the truth, and now he answered, 'Yes!' But as Devasharman set out, Vipula asked him this question: 'What forms does Indra take when he comes? What body and what sort of power? You should tell me this.' Then Devasharman told Vipula the truth about Indra's magical power: 'Indra has many and various forms of magic, and he changes them from minute to minute. He wears a diadem or holds the thunderbolt or a bow, or he wears a crown and earrings, and then in a minute he looks just like a Chandala (an outcaste hunter). He may wear a crest or matted hair or an animal skin; he may have a large body and then again he may be very fat or very thin. Tawny or dark or blue, he changes his colour and becomes ugly or handsome, young or old. Wise or stupid, short or tall, a Brahmin or Kshatriya or Vaishya or even a Shudra, he may take the form of a parrot or a crow, a goose or a cuckoo, or he may appear as a lion or tiger or elephant. He may take a divine form, or demonic, or the form of a king. Four-footed, many-formed—or he may even take the form of something like a fly or a mosquito. It is not possible for anyone to grasp him, not even the god who created this universe. When Indra has become invisible, he can be seen only with the eye of knowledge; when he has become the wind, he once again becomes the king of the gods. In this way, Indra constantly changes his forms. And so you must protect this slender-waisted woman with great care, so that the king of the gods does not lick Ruchi like an evil-minded dog licking the oblation set out for the sacrifice.'

When the sage Devasharman had said all of this, he went away to perform his sacrifice. But when Vipula heard his guru's words, he became very worried, and he wondered what he could do to protect Ruchi from the powerful king of the gods: 'How can I protect my guru's wife? For the king of the gods is a great magician, virile and hard to assault. It's not possible to conceal the ashram or this hut to protect her, because of Indra's ability to take on various forms. Indra in the form of the wind could rape my guru's wife! Therefore, I will enter Ruchi and stay there, right now. For there is no way that I am able to protect this woman through my manly powers, but I will protect her from Indra by the power of my yoga. I will enter her limbs with my limbs to protect her. If my guru should see that his wife Ruchi has been defiled, has become someone else's leavings, he would certainly curse me in anger, for he has divine knowledge and great *tapas*. But this woman cannot be protected as other men protect their beautiful women, for this king of the gods is a great magician, and so I am faced with a dilemma. My guru's command must absolutely be carried out; but to do this, I would have to perform a miracle.

'I will enter the body of my guru's wife by means of yoga; and no fault will be mine, as I have been freed from any trace of passion. Just as a traveller might live in an empty traveller's lodge on the road, in that very way today I will live in the body of my guru's wife. Just as a trembling drop of water remains on the leaf of a lotus without being attached to it, in that very same way I will live in her body, with my thoughts collected and repressed.' In this way, considering dharma in all its aspects, and with regard for his own and his guru's massive *tapas*, thinking in that way in his mind about protection and control, Vipula made a great effort. Hear what it was!

Vipula sat down next to his guru's wife as she, with her flawless limbs, was sitting there, and he distracted her with stories. Fixing his eyes on her eyes, and the beams of light from his eyes on the beams from her eyes, Vipula entered her body as the wind enters the sky. Mingling his characteristics with hers, his face with her face, the sage vanished and remained there without moving, like her shadow. Permeating the body of his guru's wife, Vipula lived there, engaged in protecting and controlling her, and she did not know he was there. All that time, until his guru finished his sacrifice and returned to his home, Vipula protected and controlled her.

Then, one day, Indra, thinking, 'This is my opportunity,' taking on a most gorgeous and highly desirable form, with unparalleled beauty, entered that ashram. He saw the body of Vipula seated there, motionless, with staring, unseeing eyes, just as if he was in a drawing. And he saw Ruchi, perfect in all her limbs, with her plump buttocks and full breasts, her eyes as broad as lotus petals, her face like a full moon. When she saw him, she suddenly wanted to stand up, for she was smitten by his beauty, and she wanted to say, 'Who are you?' But Vipula held her back, restraining her so that she could not move. Indra spoke to her in his most persuasive and flattering words: 'Know that I am Indra, come here for your sake, for your sweet smile; I am tormented by the god of love, by my desire for you. Give in to me, for too much time has already been lost.' The sage Vipula, inside the body of his guru's wife, heard Indra talking like this and saw him. Ruchi was blameless, for she was not able to stand up, nor was she able to speak, paralysed as she was by Vipula. But Vipula recognized the involuntary signs of arousal in his guru's wife, and so he held fast to her powerfully, by yoga. He bound all of her senses with the bonds of yoga.

When Indra saw that she showed no signs of emotion, he was ashamed and embarrassed, and once again he spoke to her: 'Come! Come!' She wanted to reply to Indra, but Vipula turned back her speech and stupefied her by the power of his yoga. So what came out of her lovely mouth was, 'Greetings! What is your purpose in coming here?' This was spoken in the refined speech, Sanskrit. She was ashamed and embarrassed as she said those words while she was in the power of someone else; and Indra at first was terrified and then felt very foolish. When he heard this peculiar speech of Vipula, he looked with his divine gaze, for he has a thousand eyes. And then he saw the sage moving about inside her body, inside the body of his guru's wife, like an image in a mirror. And realizing that that sage must have formidable *tapas*, Indra trembled in terror, fearing a curse.

Then Vipula let go of his guru's wife and entered his own body and said to the terrified Indra, 'You have never mastered your senses; you have an evil nature; you are nothing but your lusts, Indra. The gods and humans will not honour you for long. Have you forgotten that you were marked with the images of vaginas until Gautama freed you? I know that you have the mind of a fool, that you are fickle and uncouth. This woman is protected and controlled by me, you fool. Go back where you came from. I am not going to burn you up today with my fiery power, because I pity you. But my wise guru has terrible *tapas*, and if he saw you, you evil-minded creature, he would burn you up right away with his eye blazing with anger. Never act like this again! You must honour Brahmins, or else you and your sons and your whole entourage will be tormented by the power of Brahmins. If you behave like this because you think, "I am an immortal," you should stop, for there is nothing that cannot be achieved by *tapas*.' When Indra heard what Vipula had said, he was so ashamed that he didn't say anything at all, and simply disappeared right there.

But the very moment that Indra left, Devasharman, having completed his sacrifice as he wished, came back to his own ashram. When his guru arrived, Vipula reported to him that his blameless wife had been protected. Greeting his guru with a peaceful soul, Vipula stood fearlessly beside him as before, for his guru loved him as a cow loves her calf. When Devasharman had rested and was seated with his wife, Vipula told him all that Indra had done. And when the sage heard this, he was satisfied with Vipula, because of Vipula's good character and behaviour, and his *tapas*, and his self-control, his devotion to his guru and his firmness in dharma, caring for dharma above all. 'Bravo, bravo!' said Devasharman, congratulating his pupil, and he offered him a boon. With his guru's permission, Vipula engaged in unsurpassed *tapas*. And Devasharman and his wife wandered about in that deserted forest, with no fear of Indra.

But one day, in a lonely place, Vipula saw a pair of men dancing in a circle, holding hands. One of them quickly took a step and turned, but the other did not, and so a quarrel arose between them. One said, 'You are going too fast!' and the other said, 'No I'm not!' And the two of them said, 'No!' 'No!' to one another. As they argued in this way, a certain curse arose in their minds concerning Vipula, and so they both said, 'Whichever of the two of us has lied, may he reach in the world to come the final destination[11] of that Brahmin Vipula.' When Vipula heard this, his face sank and he thought, 'I have accomplished such terrible *tapas*, and this is my miserable punishment for it. What evil have I done to get the hateful final destination that this couple have attributed to me today?'

While Vipula was worrying about this, with his face down, his head bowed, he tried to think what evil deed he himself had committed. Then he saw six other men, filled with greed and excitement, playing with gold and silver dice. They spoke the same curse that the other couple had made, mentioning Vipula, for they said, 'Whoever among us is so greedy that he tries to cheat, let him obtain in the world beyond the very same final destination as Vipula.' When Vipula heard this curse, he could not see any violation of dharma that he himself had ever committed in the past, though he thought hard, with a burning mind. Many days and nights passed as he worried in this way, and then into his mind came the way that he had protected and guarded Ruchi. 'Mingling my characteristics with her characteristics,' he thought, 'her face with my face—I did not tell this truly to my guru.' Vipula realized that this was his misdeed, and there was no doubt about it. And he went to honour, in the proper way, his guru who loved him.

When Devasharman saw that his pupil had come back, he said to him, 'Vipula, what did you see today in the great forest?

The people there are clever, and they know about you, and about me and Ruchi too.' Vipula told him what had happened and asked, 'Who were that couple, and who were those men? Tell me about them, for they know the truth about me.' Devasharman said, 'The couple who danced in a circle were day and night, who know your evil deed. And those men who were playing dice so excitedly are the six seasons, who know your evil deed. No one should be so confident as to think, "No one knows all about me." For a man may have an evil soul in secret, but he has evil karma, and the seasons and day and night always see the man who commits evil deeds in secret. When they saw you smiling in joy, though you had not reported your actions to your guru, they spoke in the way that you heard, to remind you. Day and night know, and the seasons always know, a man's evil deeds and good deeds. They knew that, because you were afraid that you had transgressed, you did not tell me truly what you had done, and so they spoke to you. For the worlds of an evildoer would be your worlds, so long as you did not tell me what you had done.

'But as that was the only way that a badly behaved, sensual woman could be protected, you did not commit any sin. I am pleased with you! If I had seen you behave badly, I would have cursed you in anger, without a moment's hesitation. If you hadn't protected her, your curse would have been to have such a future existence as the people in the forest spoke of. But you did protect her, my son, and kept her safe for me. I am pleased with you, my child. Be well; you will go to heaven.' When Devasharman had said this to Vipula, with whom he was pleased, he rejoiced and went to heaven with his wife and with his little pupil.

[13.41–43]

3. How Bhangashvana Became a Woman

The misogynist texts that we have considered so far insist that women's desire and sexual pleasure greatly exceed those of men. The following story attempts to substantiate and document this widespread opinion. (Some tellings of the similar Greek myth of Tiresias, who became a woman for a while, made the same point.) But the statement that women are more affectionate than men, particularly towards their children, might be viewed as a competing example of philogyny. So, too, the king's confession that 'I seemed to be unsatisfied by my sons and wives and wealth' might be read as a suggestion that he actually *wanted* to be a woman, right from the start.

The otherwise unmotivated rise of enmity between the king's two sets of sons is attributed to nothing but Time, which is one translation of the Sanskrit word *kala* (from the verb *kal*, to count, cognate with the English 'calculate'), a word that means 'time', 'death', 'fate', and 'doomsday'. To signal this range of meanings, I will always capitalize the first letter.

The Text

Yudhishthira said, 'When a man and a woman unite, which of them has the greater sensual pleasure? I have my doubts about this, and you ought to explain it properly.' Bhishma said: 'They tell this ancient history about that very subject, involving an age-old enmity between Indra and Bhangashvana.'

Once upon a time, there was a most dharmic and self-controlled king named Bhangashvana. As he had no son, he performed a sacrifice for the sake of a son. But he performed the sacrifice 'In Praise of Fire' [*agnishtoma*], a sacrifice that mortals who desire a son like, but that Indra hates. A hundred powerful sons were born of the king's loins, but when Indra learned about the sacrifice, he looked for a vulnerable point in Bhangashvana. After a while, when the king was riding his horse, wandering about on a hunt, Indra thought, 'This is my opportunity,' and he confused the king so that he wandered about on his horse, not knowing what direction he was heading in. Suffering from hunger and thirst and exhaustion, the king galloped here and there, until he saw a shining lake full of fine water. Dismounting, he let his horse drink from the lake; then he tied the horse to a tree and he plunged in and bathed. He changed into a woman, and his stallion became a mare.

When he saw that he had been turned into a woman, the king was ashamed, worried, and confused. He wondered, 'But how will I mount my horse? And how will I go to the city? What will I say to my sons, and my wives, and the people of the city and the countryside? Tenderness, delicacy and bewildered timidity are the qualities of women, while the qualities of a man are athletic strength, roughness and manliness. So the sages have said who have seen the purpose and essence of dharma. Who has destroyed my manly qualities and made me a woman? And now that I am a woman, how will I be able to mount my horse again?' But then, with a great effort, the king who had become a woman mounted his horse and went back to the city.

His sons and wives and servants and the people of the city and the countryside were greatly astonished, wondering, 'What is this?' Then the king who had become a woman said: 'I went out on a hunt, closely surrounded by my entourage of strong men. But I was deluded by fate and wandered off until I entered a horrible forest. Half out of my mind, suffering from thirst, I saw a lake that looked beautiful. I dived into it and became a woman. This must have been fated, as I seemed to be unsatisfied by my sons and wives and wealth.' And then the king who had become a woman said to her sons, 'Enjoy the kingdom in all happiness, my little sons; I am going to the forest.' And the king consecrated her hundred sons in the kingship and went to the forest.

A man of *tapas* happened to encounter the woman Bhangashvana in an ashram, and he fathered another hundred sons in Bhangashvana. Then she took those sons and said to her former sons, 'You are the sons I bore in masculinity, and these hundred sons I bore in femininity. My sons, enjoy the kingdom in unity and brotherhood.' But when Indra saw them enjoying the kingdom in the spirit of brotherhood, he was flooded with jealous anger, brooding and thinking, 'I have done this king a favour, not an injury.'

Then Indra took on the form of a Brahmin and went to the city and caused a break between the king's sons. He said, 'There is no true brotherhood between brothers even when they are the sons of a single father. The gods and demons quarrelled for the sake of a kingdom, even though both the gods and the demons were the sons of the sage Kashyapa. But you are the sons of Bhangashvana, and those others are the sons of the man of *tapas*; and the sons of the man of *tapas* are enjoying *your* paternal kingdom.'

When Indra had broken them into factions, they fell to fighting with one another. And when the woman Bhangashvana heard about that, she was deeply distressed, and she lamented. Indra disguised himself as a Brahmin and asked her, 'What grief is making you weep in such pain? You have a lovely face.' The woman said, piteously, 'Good Brahmin, my two hundred sons have been destroyed by fate. I used to be a king, and had a hundred sons, handsome and brave. But one day I went on a hunt and got lost in a deep forest; I dove into a lake and became a woman. I established my sons in the kingdom and then went back to the forest. As a woman I then had another hundred sons by a man of *tapas*; they were born in the ashram, and I brought them to the city. But an enmity arose between the two groups, through the power of Time, and that is why I am grieving, overwhelmed by destiny.'

When Indra saw how unhappy the woman was, he spoke roughly to her: 'In the past I was unbearably unhappy, my good lady, and you were the cause of my unhappiness, because you insulted me with a sacrifice that Indra hates. I am Indra, you evil-minded woman, and you have incurred my hatred.' When the king saw that it was Indra, she touched Indra's feet with her head and said, 'Have mercy! That sacrifice was made in the desire to have a son. You should forgive me for that.' She pleased Indra by falling at his feet, and he offered her a boon: 'Which of your sons should live? Tell me. Those who were born of you when you were a woman or when you were a man?'

The woman of *tapas* then joined her hands in respect and said to Indra, 'Those who were born of me when I was a woman—let them live, Indra!' Indra was astonished and delighted, and he asked the woman again, 'Your sons that you begat as a man, why should you hate them? And how can you have the greater affection for those who were born of you when you were a woman?' The woman said: 'The affection of a woman is greater than that of a man. Therefore, the sons who were born when I had been made into a woman—let them live.' Indra was pleased and said, 'Let *all* of your sons live here, as you have spoken the truth. And choose any boon you wish, and I will be pleased to grant it to you—manhood, or womanhood, whatever you desire from me.'

The woman said: 'Womanhood is what I choose, Indra, if

you are pleased to grant it.' Indra replied to the woman, 'How can you reject manhood and prefer womanhood?' The king who had become a woman replied, 'In sexual union with a man, women always have greater pleasure. And that is why, Indra, I choose to be a woman. I have greater sexual pleasure in being a woman, truly; I am quite satisfied being a woman. Let me go.' 'So be it,' said Indra, and went back to the triple heaven.

And so the pleasure of women is said to be greater.

[13.12]

4. How Satyavati's Mother Corrupted Her Daughter's Pregnancy

This is a much retold story, and I have included two different versions in this collection, one from Book Twelve (the *Shanti Parvan*) and one from Book Thirteen (the *Anushanasa Parvan*).

Let us begin with the *Shanti Parvan* version of the story.

4a. How Richika's Mother-in-Law and Wife Conceived the Wrong Sons

Many of the stories that Bhishma tells Yudhishthira are designed to console him as he mourns for the death of so many of his relatives and companions. So, too, in the *Shanti Parvan*, Krishna tells Yudhishthira this story of the ancestry of Parashu Rama ('Rama with the Axe', always to be distinguished from the Rama of the *Ramayana*) and, more particularly, the story of the subsequent survival of the lineage of all the kings whom Parashu Rama murders, to point the same encouraging moral about the non-finality of death.

But this story of the birth of the spectacularly destructive Parashu Rama, from Jamadagni the son of Satyavati, also has a lot to say about meddling women. No name is given here for the wicked mother of Satyavati (the wife of Richika), but elsewhere she is said to be an Apsaras named Adrika. Whoever she is, she starts all the trouble by mixing the classes of the sons who are to be born of her and those to be born of her daughter. In the general slaughter that eventually ensues, a few women actually act for the good of the human race by protecting some of their sons, but once again it is the wickedness of women that prevails, or more precisely, the wickedness of men excited by women. For, 'in the absence of Kshatriyas, the Shudras and Vaishyas, doing whatever they wanted to, made sexual advances to the wives of the leading Brahmins', and once again the earth is almost destroyed by the evils of miscegenation, until the race of Kshatriyas is finally restored to establish the moral law. For, as we will see later, in the stories explaining and justifying kingship, without Kshatriyas the world inevitably descends into moral chaos.

This myth also accounts for another famous character who violates the basic class barriers of classical Hinduism: Vishvamitra, who is born a Kshatriya and becomes a great Brahmin (in a famous story not told here, despite Bhishma's promise to tell it to Yudhishthira).

The plot of this story turns upon a woman's wilful confusion of two *charus*. A *charu* is a pudding made of milk and rice, blessed by a Brahmin and fed to a woman to ensure that she has a male child. Yet the trouble really begins earlier, with a king, Gadhi, who gives his daughter in marriage not to a man of his own class, a Kshatriya, as he should, but to a Brahmin. As Gadhi is an incarnation of Indra, he may just be up to mischief as usual, but, as we will see in other stories, many kings give their daughters in marriage to Brahmins, though not always with such disastrous results. It may also be that, as Gadhi wanted a son but got a daughter instead, the curse of the 'wrong' gender is carried over to the next generation, where it becomes the curse of the 'wrong' class.

The Text

Krishna said: 'Listen to what I heard when the great sages told stories about the birth of Parashu Rama. And just as the Kshatriyas whom Parashu Rama killed were reborn in the dynasties of kings, so, all the more, will those slain in the Bharata War be reborn.'

King Kushika knew dharma, and he engaged in fierce *tapas*, thinking, 'May I have a son who will be the unconquered ruler of the three worlds.' When Indra saw the king engaged in such fierce *tapas*, knowing that he was capable of begetting such a son, Indra himself went there and became the son of Kushika, known as Gadhi.

Now, King Gadhi gave his daughter Satyavati in marriage to Richika, the son of a Brahmin sage. Delighted, Richika cooked a *charu* in order to have a son for himself, and he also cooked a *charu* for his father-in-law, Gadhi. Richika summoned his wife, Satyavati, and said, 'This *charu* is for you to eat, and this one is for your mother. She will give birth to a brilliant son, a Kshatriya who will destroy all the Kshatriyas in the world. But this other *charu*, for you, will make your son the best of Brahmins, steadfast, self-controlled, and rich in *tapas*.' When Richika had said this to his wife, he went back into the forest, dedicating himself to *tapas*.

Now, at this very time, King Gadhi went on a pilgrimage, with his wife, and they arrived at Richika's ashram. Satyavati took the pair of *charus*, but she failed to keep in mind her husband's words, and in her excitement, she presented them both to her mother. And her mother, unknown to the daughter, gave her the *charu* that was intended for herself, the mother, and the mother made her daughter's *charu* her own. And so Satyavati conceived an embryo that was to be the death of the Kshatriyas, a creature with a hideous, blazing form.

When Richika saw his wife through the yoga of his meditation, he said to her, 'My dear, your mother has cheated you, by exchanging the *charus*. For your son will be born with great strength and will do cruel deeds, while your brother [that is, your mother's son] will be born rich in *tapas*. This is not the wish that I had in mind for you, my dear. But, because of the *charu* and your mother, your son will do terrible things.' Satyavati said, 'You can create whatever worlds you desire, but what about me? Let me have a decent son with a peaceful soul.' Richika said: 'I have never before said an untrue word, even in trifling matters. Then how could I do what you ask, when I kindled a fire with all the mantras needed to prepare that *charu*?' Satyavati said, 'Granted, but let our *grandson*, yours and mine, be terrible like that; and let my *son* be decent, with a peaceful soul.' Richika said, 'I make no distinction between a son and a grandson. Let it be just as you have said.'

And so Satyavati gave birth to the Brahmin Jamadagni, who had a peaceful soul and delighted in *tapas*. And Gadhi's Kshatriya heir, Satyavati's mother's son, was Vishvamitra. But Jamadagni begat a most terrible son, Parashu Rama, who mastered all the sciences and was a supreme archer but was like a blazing fire when he killed all the Kshatriyas.

Now, at this very time, Arjuna Kartavirya was born, a powerful and energetic Kshatriya with a thousand arms. With the power of his own arms and his weapons in battle, he burnt the entire earth, all of the seven continents, and the towns, until he burnt the ashram of the sage Vasishtha. Then Vasishtha, in anger, cursed Arjuna Kartavirya: 'Since in your delusion you did not spare this ashram of mine but burnt it, therefore Parashu Rama will cut off all your thousand arms in battle.' And because of that curse, the powerful, cruel, and arrogant sons of Arjuna Kartavirya stole the calf of Jamadagni's cow, though Arjuna Kartavirya did not know about this. Then Parashu Rama, the manly son of Jamadagni, cut off Arjuna Kartavirya's many arms and sent the bellowing calf out of Arjuna Kartavirya's inner citadel back to Jamadagni's ashram. Arjuna Kartavirya's sons then lost their minds; imprudently, they went to Jamadagni's ashram and separated Jamadagni's head from his body with their sharp-tipped arrows.

At this time, Parashu Rama had gone out of the ashram to gather fuel. When he returned and saw that his father, Jamadagni, had been murdered, he was unable to brook his anger and was overcome by great vengeful wrath. He took up his weapon and swore to remove all the Kshatriyas from the earth. Quickly he attacked and killed all the sons and grandsons of Kartavirya, every single one. Then he killed thousands of other Kshatriyas and turned the mud of the earth to blood. And when he had made the earth empty of all Kshatriyas, he was overcome by great pity and went into the woods.

But he had actually left alive hundreds of powerful infant Kshatriyas, and after thousands of years, they grew up and became the lords of the earth. Once again, he quickly murdered them, powerful though they were, for they were children; and as each embryo was born, again and again he killed them. But the Kshatriya women protected some of their sons, and the earth was once again pervaded by those who had been hidden in the womb. Twenty-one times Parashu Rama emptied the earth of Kshatriyas, but eventually the sage Kashyapa banished Parashu Rama to the shore of the Southern ocean, making the earth a safe place for Brahmins.

However, in the absence of Kshatriyas, the Shudras and Vaishyas, doing whatever they wanted to, made sexual advances to the wives of the leading Brahmins. For when there is no king in the world of living creatures, the powerless are oppressed by the more powerful, and no one has lordship over his possessions. Then, after a while, the Earth entered the watery underworld, for she was not being protected properly by the Kshatriyas, who maintain dharma. As the Earth was sinking into the water, she begged Kashyapa to give her strong-armed Kshatriyas for her protectors. She said, 'I have hidden some mighty Kshatriyas. Let them protect me!' Kashyapa gathered together those whom the Earth had honoured for their heroism. He anointed them as Kshatriya kings. Their sons and grandsons established the present dynasties.

[12.49]

4b. How Richika's Wife and Mother-in-Law Conceived the Wrong Sons

The story of the mixed-up *charus* takes on interesting variations in the *Anushasana Parvan* telling, which acknowledges from the start that the original problem is not with the women but with the men: Gadhi, being a king, should not have let his daughter marry a Brahmin, as he knows full well, though his objection is explicitly said to be not to the prospective bridegroom's class but to his lack of money. Gadhi tries in vain to set the would-be bridegroom an impossible task, but here too Gadhi is at fault, for the bride price given by the groom is considered dishonourable in a tradition that generally insists instead on a dowry given by the bride.

The mother in this version of the story is even more explicitly wicked than she was in the *Shanti Parvan*. She lies outright when she tells her daughter that Gadhi *wanted* her to switch the *charus*. And now she goes to far greater lengths to make sure that she gets the son she wants, the great sage Vishvamitra, whose transition from Kshatriya to Brahmin is now at least alluded to, though still not narrated, and who is still the main persona in the story, from Yudhishthira's standpoint. The implication is that the ambivalent gender of the *charus* accounts for the ambivalence of Vishvamitra's class status. (Nothing is said here about the violent Parashu Rama, born of Satyavati's son Jamadagni). In this telling, some good as well as evil eventually comes out of the complex connivings of Richika's mother-in-law.

The Text

Yudhishthira asked, 'If it is hard for the other three classes to become Brahmins, how did the Kshatriya Vishvamitra become a Brahmin? I wish to know this; tell me this truly.' Bhishma said, 'It has been heard how, once in the past, Vishvamitra became not just a Brahmin but even a great Brahmin sage. Hear now about his birth.'

King Gadhi, the son of the great King Kushika, had no son, but when he was living in the forest, a beautiful daughter was born to him, named Satyavati. The Brahmin Richika chose her as his bride, but Gadhi did not want to give her to Richika, thinking, 'He is poor!' Richika started to leave, because he had been rejected, but Gadhi called him back and said, 'Give me a bride price, and then you will obtain my daughter.' Richika said, 'What should I give you as bride price for your daughter? Tell me, and do not hesitate or hold anything back.' Gadhi said, 'Give me a thousand horses white as moonbeams, swift as the wind, and each with one black ear.'

Richika went to Varuna, lord of the waters, and said, 'I beg you to give me a thousand horses white as moonbeams, swift as the wind, and each with one black ear.' 'Yes,' said Varuna to Richika. 'Wherever you wish for the horses, there they will appear.' As soon as Richika thought of those horses white as moonbeams, swift as the wind, and each with one black ear, a thousand of them stood up out of the water of the Ganges. Then Richika, delighted, gave the thousand horses to Gadhi as the bride price, and Gadhi, amazed but fearing the Brahmin's curse, adorned his daughter and gave her to Richika. Richika took her hand in the marriage ritual, and she was delighted to accept him for her husband.

Richika was so pleased by her behaviour that he did her the favour of offering her a boon. The girl reported everything to her mother, and the mother said to her daughter, who stood looking down, 'My daughter, your husband should do a favour for me, too. He has great *tapas* and is quite capable of granting a son.' Then Satyavati went quickly and reported to Richika all of this that her mother wanted to have done. Richika said to her, 'Both you and she will, each, bring forth a virtuous son. But do not let your mother ask for anything else. You, my lovely one, will give birth to a son proud of his virtues; and your glorious brother [i.e. your mother's son] will perpetuate our Kshatriya family line. When you and she have bathed after your menstrual periods, you must embrace a fig tree, and she must embrace a banyan,[12] and both of you will get what you desire. Here are a pair of *charus*, purified by mantras; you and she must each take and eat one, and then both of you will get sons.'

Satyavati, rejoicing, reported to her mother what Richika had said, and she also told her about the two *charus*. Then Satyavati's mother said to her, 'My daughter, as I bow my head to you as a suppliant, do what I say. The *charu* that your husband gave to you, purified by mantras, is the one you must give to me, and you take mine. And let us also make an exchange of the trees—if you take my word, your mother's word, as authoritative. It is clear that precisely what your husband wanted done will be done in this matter; therefore, let your *charu* be mine, and your tree be mine. And think how your brother may become preeminent.' Satyavati and her mother acted in this way, and both of them became pregnant.

But when Richika saw that his wife Satyavati had become pregnant, he was disappointed, and he said to her, 'It is quite clear that your *charus* were exchanged, and it is equally clear that the trees were also exchanged. I had placed all that is Brahmin in your *charu* and placed the entire power of the Kshatriyas in her *charu*. You would have given birth to a Brahmin famed throughout the three worlds for his virtues, and she to a distinguished Kshatriya; that is what I did. But since you and your mother made the exchange in that way, your mother will give birth to an outstanding Brahmin, and you will give birth to a Kshatriya who will do terrible deeds. For what you did out of your affection for your mother was not good.'

When Satyavati heard this, she fell to the ground, tormented by sorrow, like a gorgeous vine that had been cut down. When she regained consciousness, she touched the ground with her head and said to her husband, 'Forgive me, forgive your wife; have mercy, and let me not have a Kshatriya son. If it please you, let my grandson be the one who does terrible deeds, but let it not be my son; please grant me this boon.' 'So be it!' he said to his wife. And so she gave birth to the glorious Brahmin Jamadagni. And Satyavati's mother gave birth to Vishvamitra, who was born a Kshatriya but became a Brahmin sage and the founder of a dynasty of Brahmins.

[13.4]

5. How Ashtavakra Resisted Seduction by an Old Woman

The hero of this story, Ashtavakra, 'a man crooked in eight ways', is also the victim of a miscarriage of *charus*. The old story tells us that a king died without an heir, and one of his two wives ate a *charu* consecrated to make her pregnant, while the other wife 'acted the part of a man' with her. She became pregnant, but the child had no bones, because the man contributes, from his semen, the white and hard parts of the embryo, bones and sinews, while the woman contributes, from her blood, the red and soft parts, blood and flesh.[13] Ashtavakra was therefore grotesquely deformed, which is not explicitly mentioned in this story but is perhaps not irrelevant. For the text tells us that the old woman whom he encounters is deformed in every limb, as other texts say of Ashtavakra himself. But she is merely disguised as an old hag; she is really a beautiful goddess, the incarnation of Disha, the Northern Quarter of the compass, the earth and the sky.

At the start of the text, Bhishma justifies his low opinion of women by asserting that the Vedas state that 'women are false'. The Vedas (sometimes just called 'the Veda') are the oldest texts of Hinduism, centuries older even than the *Mahabharata*, and are often cited as the ultimate authority for any important belief or practice. We will encounter, in other stories, too, this appeal to the Vedas' ultimate authority, one that is hard to dispute, as few people, even in ancient India, were able to read the difficult archaic Sanskrit of the Vedas.

The woman whom Ashtavakra encounters is, unlike the other women in the narratives in this collection, independent of any man and unafraid of the sage's curse. But this anomaly is explained when, at the end, she turns out to be not a woman, after all, but a goddess.

The Text

Yudhishthira asked Bhishma: 'Since women are false, as we read in the Vedas, why do the texts speak of the shared dharma of husband and wife?' Bhishma replied: 'On this subject they tell this ancient history about the conversation between Ashtavakra and Disha.'

Once upon a time, the Brahmin Ashtavakra, who had great *tapas*, wished to marry the daughter of the noble sage Vadanya. Her name was Suprabha, and her beauty was unmatched on earth, as were her virtues, her good nature, her excellent behaviour, and her gracefulness. The moment she looked at him she stole his mind and heart. Vadanya said to him, 'My daughter can be given to you, but listen to me. Go, first, to the auspicious Northern Quarter and look there.' Ashtavakra said, 'What should I see there? Tell me, and I will do what you tell me to do.' Vadanya said, 'Go past the Himalayas, until you see a blue forest, and in it you will see a woman. She is old now and has been engaged in *tapas*. You must see her and work hard to honour her. And when you have seen her and returned, then you will take my daughter's hand in marriage.'

Ashtavakra replied, 'So be it! I will certainly journey there, just as you have said. And you, sir, must be true to your word.'

And so he set out to the North, to the Himalayas. Eventually he looked all around him and began to worry, 'Where might I find a place to live?' Then he saw a door, and he went up to it and said, 'Whoever may be here, know that I am a guest who has arrived.' Then seven beautiful maidens came out of the house. Whatever maiden he looked at, she stole his mind and heart. He could not control his mind and heart, and he grew faint. He tried to remain firm, but then the lovely women said, 'Good sir, please enter.' Filled with curiosity about those beautiful women and about the building, he entered the house.

There he saw an old woman seated on a bed, wearing a white garment and a great deal of jewellery. 'How do you do?' he said, and she replied, 'Welcome!' Then she rose to greet him and said, 'Please sit down.' Ashtavakra said, 'Let all the women go to their own homes, and let just one attend me, one who is very wise and very tranquil; let all the others go wherever they wish.' At this, the young women circled the sage to the right, in the formal ritual of taking leave, and went out of the house. Only the old woman stayed there, lying on a gorgeous bed. He approached her and said, 'You too should go to sleep, my good woman, for the night is passing.' She engaged him in conversation until he lay down on a second magnificent bed.

Then she began to tremble in all her limbs, pretending that this was caused by the cold, and she climbed into the great sage's bed. He said to her, 'Welcome! Welcome!' But she clasped him passionately to her bosom with her two arms. When she saw that he showed no emotion at all, like a wooden wall, she was miserable. She suffered for a while in silence, and then she tried to begin a conversation: 'Brahmin, women cannot help but indulge their desires, but men have self-control. I am drunk with desire; make love with me as I make love with you. Get aroused, great sage, and unite with me. Embrace me, for I am tortured with violent desire for you. This is the fruit won by your *tapas*; from the moment I saw you, I desired you. You are master over this house, and this forest, and everything else that you see. I will give you everything you desire; make love with me in this lovely forest that will yield the fruits of all desires. I will be in your power; make love with me and you will enjoy all the pleasures of the gods and of mortal men. For women have no duty and no reward beyond that of uniting with a man. Women goaded by desire act according to their own will; they are not burnt even when they walk over very hot sands.'

Ashtavakra said: 'My good woman, never, under any circumstances, would I go to bed with the wife of another man. According to the dharma texts, intimate contact with the wife of another man is filthy. My good woman, I swear truly: you must know that I desire to settle down with a wife. Since one must have offspring for the sake of dharma, I will have sons; there is no doubt about that. But I have no experience of worldly matters. You must recognize this dharma, and knowing this, you must desist.'

The woman said, 'Women do not love the god of Wind, or Fire, or Water, or any of the other thirty-three gods, as much as they love Kama, the god of Desire; for the very nature of women is sexual pleasure. Just as only one woman in a thousand ever arrives here, even so among a hundred thousand women, only one is devoted to her husband. These women do not care about their father or their family or their mother, nor about their brothers or their husband or their sons or their brothers-in-law. Carried away by sexual frivolity, they destroy the family [*kula*] just as rivers destroy their banks [*kUla*]. Brahma used to speak about the stupid vices in these stupid women.'

Then the sage, ever single-minded, replied to the woman, 'Never mind the desire for pleasure. What else should be done? Tell me.' The woman replied, 'Good sir, you will see this, depending on the place and the time. Live here for a while and you will do what is to be done.' Ashtavakra said to her, 'So be it. I will certainly live here as long as you have the strength for it.' Then he looked at the woman, who was afflicted by old age, and he became seriously worried and distressed. For no matter whatever limb of hers he looked at, her form confounded his gaze and he found no pleasure in it. 'She is the goddess of this house,' he thought, 'but somehow she has been deformed by a curse. I cannot understand the cause of this now.' As he was worrying about this, wanting to know the meaning of it, his mind all stirred up, the day came to an end.

Then the woman said, 'Good sir, see that the sun is now touched by the clouds of sunset. What can I do for you?' He replied, 'I will restrain my senses and my speech and perform the twilight ritual. Bring me water here for my bath.' The woman replied, 'So be it,' and she brought heavenly oil and a gown for his bath. With his permission, she rubbed all his limbs—all of them—with the oil. Then she brought him into the bathing room and gently seated him on a beautiful new seat. She bathed him tenderly, with skilled hands. The extremely pleasant water and her gentle hands made him forget the time, and the whole night passed that way without him noticing it. When he got up, he was astonished to see the sun rising in the eastern sky. The thought struck him: 'What delusion can this be?' He worshipped the sun and said to her, 'What shall I do?' She gave him food that tasted like ambrosia, but it was so sweet that he could not eat much of it. And so the whole day passed and again it was evening. Then the woman urged him, 'Sleep!' and she prepared two divine beds for him and for her.

Ashtavakra said, 'My good woman, my mind is not attracted to the wives of other men. Get up. Go to sleep and stop this.' Though he repulsed her like this firmly, she replied, 'If you see a sin in the wives of other men, then just take my hand now (in a ceremony of marriage) as I touch you and there will be no vice; I am telling you the truth. I am independent, attached to no man; this would be no perversion of your dharma. I am independent; if there is any violation of dharma, let it be in me.' He said, 'How can you be independent? Tell me the reason for this. Women have no independence. This was Brahma's decision: A woman does not deserve independence. There is not a single woman in this world who should have independence. Her father protects her when she is a girl, and her husband protects her when she is a young woman, her sons when she is an old woman. No woman should have independence.'

The woman said, 'I have been chaste since I was a young girl; I am a virgin; there is no doubt about this. Do not doubt me; do not lose your confidence in me. Sexual desire is tormenting me; you will commit a violation of dharma if you do not pleasure me. See how devoted I am.' 'All sorts of vices lead a man astray according to his desires,' he replied. 'But I am always strong in my self-control. My good woman, go back to your own bed.'

The woman said, 'Grant me this favour, as I have fallen on the ground in supplication. Be my refuge.'

[*Here she apparently changes her form and appears to him as a beautiful young girl.*]

Ashtavakra said, 'As you feel towards me, so I feel towards you; and as I feel towards you, so you feel towards me. But this promise that I made to the sage—would this not be an obstacle to the truth?' And he thought to himself, 'What would be best for me? For this maiden has come to me wearing divine ornaments and garments. What is her real form? How is it that then she was worn out by old age and now she has the form of a young maiden? And what will be her ultimate form? But I will never deviate from my fortitude.'

Yudhishthira said, 'How is it that that woman did not fear the curse of such a powerful sage? And how did he turn away? Please tell me.' Bhishma said:

Ashtavakra asked her, 'How do you change your form? Don't lie. And tell me about your desire for a Brahmin.' The woman said, 'This desire is in heaven as it is here on earth. Listen carefully to all of this. Know that I am Disha, the Northern Quarter. Now you have seen the weakness of women. And you have conquered the worlds by refusing to swerve from the right path. I contrived this test of your firmness, for the fever for sex torments even old women. But today Brahma is satisfied with you, and so are Indra and the other gods, satisfied by what you have accomplished here. For Vadanya, the Brahmin father of the young girl, sent you here to be instructed, and I have done all that. Now you will go home safely, and without fatigue. You will get the girl and she will have sons. You asked me about desire, and I gave you the answer. You have done a good thing; now go. What else do you wish to hear?'

When he heard her words, Ashtavakra cupped his hands to his head to honour her and stood there; she gave him permission to depart, and he went back home. When he got home, he rested and honoured his people, and then he went, in all propriety, to Vadanya, who asked him what he had seen. Ashtavakra told him, gladly: 'When you gave me permission to leave, I set out for the North and I saw a great divinity. I heard what she said and have returned home. She gave me permission to tell you, too.' Vadanya said to him, 'Accept my daughter, for you are most worthy to receive her.' Ashtavakra said, 'Yes!' and rejoiced to accept that glorious maiden as his wife. He lived with her in his own ashram and was very happy there.

[13.19]

6. How Ahalya Sent Uttanka to the Underworld to Get Earrings

The woman in this story is Ahalya, notorious for having deceived her husband, the sage Gautama, with the god Indra, thus inventing adultery. The many texts that tell the story usually tell us that Ahalya was punished severely, cursed to become invisible or to be turned to stone.[14] She occupies in Hindu mythology something like the position of Jezebel in the Hebrew Bible. In the text we are about to consider, however, Ahalya, the paradigmatic evil woman, merely sends an innocent student on a dangerous and frivolous assignment. Here, Ahalya stands in contrast both with the guru's innocent daughter and with Queen Madayanti, who, though a cannibal's wife, is generous with her jewellery. Again we have these good-and-evil women, and a variant of the Indian eternal love triangle—the old guru, the beautiful young wife, and his handsome young disciple (*chela*), a sure recipe for disaster—that we first encountered in the tale of Vipula and Ruchi. But now that problem, at least, is sidestepped by giving the guru, in addition to a gorgeous and frivolous wife, a gorgeous and virtuous daughter for the disciple to marry. And in this text, the disciple and the guru's wife carefully address one another as 'mother' and 'son'. Indeed, the problematic force of love in the triangle now seems to be not the disciple's love for the guru's wife but the guru's excessive love for his disciple.

Like Richika, Uttanka encounters a magical black-and-white horse, now not a white horse with a black ear (as in the story of Richika) but a black horse with a white tail. This time the horse turns out to be an incarnate god, Fire, who saves the hero from the Nagas, magical cobras who inhabit the watery underworld and are, as snakes, the traditional enemy of horses, and, as water-dwellers, the enemy of fire.

This tale is told in the outermost frame of the *Mahabharata*, where the story (about Yudhishthira and Bhishma and Krishna and all the others) is narrated by a bard (named Vaisampayana) to King Janamejaya, the descendant of Yudhishthira.

The Text

When King Janamejaya asked what sort of tapas Uttanka had, the bard replied:

Uttanka amassed great *tapas*. He was devoted to his guru, Gautama, and to no one else. And Gautama was most pleased with Uttanka; of all his many pupils, he loved Uttanka best, because of Uttanka's self-control and purity and energy and proper behaviour. Gautama allowed thousands of his pupils to depart, but because he was so fond of Uttanka, he did not wish to give him permission to leave. After a while, old age overtook Uttanka, but he was such a devoted calf to his guru, he did not realize it.

Then one day Uttanka went to fetch firewood, and he started to carry away a great weight of wood. But he was so exhausted and starving that he was overwhelmed by that great burden and dropped the wood on the ground. His silvery matted locks became caught in the wood, and he fell to the ground with the wood. Overwhelmed by hunger, he realized that he had grown old, and he began to weep with sobs of misery.

Now, the guru's daughter had beautiful hips and large eyes like lotus petals. She caught Uttanka's tears in her hand, by her father's command, and bowed her head, for she knew dharma. But the tear drops burnt her hands, and she let them fall to the ground. Gautama said to Uttanka, 'My son, why is your mind overwhelmed by grief here today? Tell me.' Uttanka said, 'My thoughts were always on you, and I always wanted to do what would please you. I was so full of devotion to you and so concerned for your feelings that I didn't realize that I had grown old, without ever knowing happiness. I have lived with you for hundreds of years, but you never gave me permission to leave, though you gave that permission to hundreds and thousands of pupils younger than me.'

Gautama said, 'A very long time has elapsed, though I didn't realize it, because I was so fond of you and you were so eager to serve your guru. But if it is your wish to leave, accept my permission and go home without delay.' Uttanka said, 'What can I give you as the parting gift to the guru? Tell me. Once I have given this to you, I will take my leave from you and go.' Gautama said, 'Good people say that the true payment to gurus is their satisfaction. I have been entirely satisfied by your behaviour. If you were today a young man of sixteen, I would give you my daughter to be your own wife. There is no other woman who is worthy to serve you.' And at that, Uttanka became a young man and accepted that glorious woman as his wife.

When his guru had given him permission to leave, Uttanka said to the guru's wife, Ahalya, 'What can I give you for the sake of the guru? Command me. I wish to do a favour for you even if it costs me my life's breaths, or all my wealth. By means of my *tapas* I will bring back whatever is hard to get in this world, even if it is some marvellous gem. I have no doubt about that.' Ahalya said, 'I have always been fully satisfied with you, my son, just as he has been. My little son, please go wherever you wish, and that will be your fulfilment of your debt.' But Uttanka spoke again, and said, 'Command me, mother, for I must do a favour for you.' Finally, Ahalya said, 'Soudasa's wife is known to have a pair of divine earrings. If you bring them to me, that would be a good deed done for the sake of your guru.' Uttanka promised to do it and went to bring them back, to do a favour for his guru's wife.

Now, Soudasa had been cursed to become a man-eating Rakshasa, but Uttanka went to him to beg for the jewelled earrings. When Gautama said to his wife, 'Why don't I see Uttanka today?' and she told him that he had gone to get the earrings, Gautama said to her, 'It was not right for you to do this. For that king has been cursed and will surely kill Uttanka.' Ahalya said, 'I didn't know that, when I ordered Uttanka to do this for me today. But surely by your favour no danger will come to him.' And Gautama replied to his wife, 'Let it be so!'

Uttanka saw King Soudasa in a deserted forest. The king was terrible to see, his long beard smeared with human blood. But as Uttanka did not tremble, the king stood up and said to him, 'How fortunate that you came to me just when I am ready to break my fast and was hunting for food.' Uttanka said, 'Your majesty, I have come here while engaged in a task for my guru, and wise men say that a person doing something for his guru should not be harmed.' The king said, 'I can't let you go today, because I am hungry.' Uttanka said, 'So be it. Let's make an agreement. When I have accomplished what I need to do for my guru, I will come back and put myself in your power. I have heard that what I seek for my guru belongs to you, and I beg you for it. For you give jewels to the head Brahmins everywhere; you are a generous donor, and you should know that I am a fit person to receive generosity here on earth. When I have received what you have and delivered it to my guru, I will come back and put myself in your power. I promise you this truly; I have never told a lie before, even in trivial matters, so why should it be different now?' Soudasa said, 'If I have what you want to give to your guru, and if I am a person from whom you can receive something, tell me about that now.'

Uttanka said, 'You have always been a person from whom I can receive something, and so I have come to you to beg for a pair of earrings.' Soudasa said, 'My wife Madayanti is very fond of those earrings. Choose something else, and I will give it to you.' Uttanka said, 'Enough of your excuses. Give me the earrings and be true to your word.' The king replied to Uttanka, 'Go and tell the queen from me, "Give!" Doubtless, when she herself has heard this from you, speaking for me, she will smile sweetly and give you the earrings.' Uttanka said, 'Where is your wife? Can I see her? But why don't you yourself go to your wife?' Soudasa said, 'You will see her now by a waterfall in the forest.'

Uttanka went and saw Madayanti and told her what he needed. She replied, 'So be it. You are not lying. But you should give me some sort of sign of recognition. These earrings of mine are divine, and the gods and Yakshas and the great serpents, the Nagas, always want to steal them by some means or other, and so they are always watching for opportunities. If the jewels are dropped on the ground, the serpents will steal them. The Yakshas will get them if they are worn with dirty clothes, and the gods will steal them if the wearer falls asleep. Whenever these chinks appear in the armour of those who are otherwise always unassailable, the gods and Rakshasas and Nagas carry off the earrings even from someone who is generally not careless. Gold falls out of them by day and night, and at night they outshine the stars of the constellations. They stave off hunger and thirst, as well as the danger of poison, fire and wild animals. If the person who wears them is short, they become short; whatever the wearer's measure, they adjust to that. This is what these earrings of mine are like, and why they are highly valued and famed throughout the three worlds. So bring me that sign of recognition.'

Returning to the king, Uttanka asked him for a sign of recognition, which Soudasa gave him, saying, 'Say to my wife, "I cannot bear my incarnation as a flesh-eating Rakshasa, but I cannot get any other birth. When you recognize this as my thought, give him the earrings."' When Uttanka told Soudasa's wife what her husband had said, she gave him the earrings. The king said, 'You should keep the agreement that you made with me today,' and Uttanka replied, 'I will do just that, your majesty, and come back here into your power.' But Soudasa said, 'You should never under any circumstances come into my presence, for if you come, it will certainly be the death of you.'

Then Uttanka took his leave of the king and started out to return to Ahalya. He took the divine earrings and headed with great speed back to Gautama's ashram. He wrapped the earrings in a black antelope skin just as Madayanti had told him to do to protect them. But as he was overcome by hunger, he saw a wood-apple tree heavy with fruit, and he climbed it. He tied the black antelope skin in which he had wrapped the earrings to the branches of the tree, but the cord broke and the black antelope skin fell to the ground. A Naga saw the earrings and quickly grabbed them in his mouth and went down into an anthill.

As Uttanka saw the Naga stealing the earrings, he dropped down quickly from the tree, furious and miserable. Then, picking up a stout stick, he dug up the anthill, his anger and indignation heating his limbs. Under his attack, the earth trembled greatly, oppressed by his stout stick. But as he kept digging like that into the surface of the earth, determined to find the path to the world of the Nagas, Indra came to that place in his chariot yoked with bay horses, with the thunderbolt in his hand. He saw Uttanka and said to him, 'My boy, you are not able to do this. The world of the Nagas is thousands of leagues from here; I don't think you can accomplish your undertaking with a stout stick.'

Uttanka said, 'If I can't get those earrings in the Naga world, I will give up my life's breaths right before your eyes.' When Indra was unable to change Uttanka's mind, he filled Uttanka's stick with the power of his thunderbolt, and its blows shattered the earth and made a path to the Naga world. Uttanka entered the Naga world by that path and saw it stretching for thousands of leagues. Its walls were made of gold and studded with divine jewels and pearls. He saw pools with crystal stairs leading down into them, and rivers of clear water, and many trees sheltering flocks of a variety of different birds. He saw the gate to this world, five leagues high and a hundred leagues wide. And then he became downcast and lost any hope of bringing back the earrings.

But then a black horse with a white tail, with coppery eyes, seeming to blaze with energy, said to him, 'Brahmin, blow into this anus of mine and then you will get back the earrings that the Naga took from you. Do not be disgusted in any way about this, for you used to do this in Gautama's ashram.' Uttanka said, 'How did I know you in my guru's ashram? I want to hear what I "used to do".' The horse said, 'Know that I am Agni, the blazing Fire, your guru's guru. You always worshipped me, my little calf, for your guru's sake, and blew upon the fire to make it blaze up, and therefore I will do what is best for you. Do what I said, without delay.' And so Uttanka did just as Fire had told him to do, and Fire, pleased with him, blazed up with the will to burn.

Then from the deep pores of the horse's skin, as Uttanka blew into him, a thick cloud of smoke arose, terrifying the Naga world, which resounded with cries of 'Alas!' The Nagas' houses were so obscured by smoke that they could not be distinguished, like forests and mountains covered with mist and fog. Their eyes red with smoke, overheated by the energy of the fire, the Nagas came to find out what Uttanka intended to do. When they heard what he wanted, they all honoured him in the correct way. Putting the old men and the children in front, all the Nagas cupped their hands in reverence and bowed their heads and said, 'Lord, be gracious to us.' When they had propitiated Uttanka, they brought him water to wash his feet and consecrated water to drink—and gave him the divine and extremely valuable earrings.

Then Uttanka returned quickly to his guru's home and gave the earrings to his guru's wife. That is how Uttanka traversed the three worlds for the divine jewelled earrings that had been stolen. That was the power of the sage Uttanka, who had supreme *tapas*.

[14.55]

B. Good Women

7. How the Procrastinator Saved Gautama from Killing his Wife

This unusual story even forgives a wife for committing adultery. The woman is Ahalya, the wife of the sage Gautama, whom we have encountered (in the tale of Uttanka and the earrings) as a frivolous and selfish though not particularly sexual woman. But in many other texts, Ahalya is notorious for having invented the sin of adultery, when Indra easily seduced her. That story of Ahalya's adultery is so famous that the *Shanti Parvan* version of the story that we are about to consider does not even mention her name, but merely speaks of her husband, Gautama, and 'a certain crime'. The fact that the male partner is explicitly said to be Indra makes me hazard the educated guess that Ahalya is in fact the wife—though Indra, as we have already seen, does get around, and seduces (or, in the case of Devasharman's wife Ruchi, fails to seduce) the wives of many sages.

In the tale of Vipula and Ruchi, Vipula reminds Indra that Gautama had cursed him to be marked all over with vaginas; in other texts, Gautama curses Ahalya to become invisible or to turn to stone. But in the version of the story we are about to encounter, Gautama does *not* punish his wife after she has committed adultery. In the story of Uttanka and the earrings, Gautama has a daughter; in this next story, he seems to have several sons, particularly one whom he commands to kill his mother. This son, who is called the Procrastinator (*chirakarin*, literally 'acting after a long time'), predictably procrastinates and does nothing to fulfil his father's command, torn as he is between his duty to obey his father and his duty to obey the law against matricide.[15] Finally, several days later, Gautama returns and is delighted to find that his son has disobeyed him and that his wife is still alive. Eventually, father and son go to heaven together—though not, apparently, with the woman who is their wife and mother. Yet Chirakarin's meditation on his mother provides a rare but therefore all the more precious example of Indian philogyny, in this case the love of mothers.

The Text

Yudhishthira asked, 'When someone is planning to do something, should he plan quickly or over a long time?' Bhishma replied: 'They tell this ancient history about that, concerning what happened to Chirakarin, the Man who Acted After a Long Time, the Procrastinator. For a man who considers his actions for a long time is wise and does not make mistakes in the actions he undertakes.'

The wise Chirakarin was the son of Gautama. He considered all his actions for a long time and then made his decision. He stayed awake for a long time, considering his actions for a long time, and then slept. And because he took so long to do the things he did, he was called Chirakarin, the Procrastinator. But as people—themselves light-minded, and lacking farsightedness—perceived him as lazy, they said he was stupid.

Now, when a certain crime had been committed,[16] Chirakarin's father, passing over his other sons, and full of anger, said to him, 'Kill this mother of yours.' Chirakarin—because of his own nature, because he always took a long time—thought about it for a long time before he finally said, 'Yes.' And then Gautama went away to the forest to generate *tapas*, leaving his wife and his son in a solitary place.

But then Chirakarin continued to worry: 'How can I obey my father's command? But how can I kill my mother? How can I avoid plunging into this false illusion of dharma, as if I were not a good man? A father's command is the highest dharma; but it is my own dharma to protect my mother. A son is by nature not independent; but how can this not do me harm? There is no shade like a mother; there is no protection like a mother. A man is called a husband because he supports his wife and protects her. If he ceases to have those virtues, he is not a husband, not a supporter or protector. And therefore a woman does not commit a crime; her husband is the one who commits the crime. Adultery is a great sin, but it is the man who commits the crime. They say that the father is a collection of all the gods in one place, but, because of her loving affection, the mother is a collection of the gods and also all the mortals.' And so forth and so on.

As he debated within himself in this way a great deal, because he always took a long time, a long period of time passed. And then his father came to him. All the time that Gautama had engaged in *tapas*, he was deliberating about his wife's transgression of the established order. Tormented by misery, shedding many tears, finally, by the grace of the fortitude that came from his knowledge of the scriptures, Gautama was overcome by regret for the past. He thought, 'Indra, the lord of the three worlds, came to my ashram. He had taken the form of a Brahmin and the manner of a guest. My wife conciliated him with words and honoured him with the rites of welcome, and she received him with water for his feet, the water for a guest, in the proper manner. And she said to him, "I am dependent upon someone else. I will conduct myself prudently." In this unfortunate incident, the transgression was not the woman's. And so, neither the woman, nor I myself, nor the traveller who was Indra, the lord of the three worlds, committed a transgression of dharma. It was the carelessness of both of them, the intoxication, that transgressed. Those who hold back their semen in chastity have said that jealousy causes trouble. It was jealousy that hurled me into an ocean of bad deeds in which I sank down. Who will save me, now that I have killed a virtuous woman, a wife whom I should have supported but whom I punished because of my own excessive attachment to her?

'But I gave the order to the noble-minded Chirakarin. If he should be true to his name today, and take a long time, he might save me from hell! Little Chirakarin, good for you! Good for you, Little Chirakarin! If you take a long time today, then you are my Little Chirakarin. Save me and your mother and all the *tapas* that I have amassed, and save yourself from all the misdeeds that would otherwise cause you to fall. Be truly Little Chirakarin today! Taking a long time is born in you, natural to you, because of your long-lasting wisdom; make that quality bear fruit today! Be Little Chirakarin today! Your mother kept you in her womb for a long time, hoping for you for a long time. Make fruitful that quality of taking a long time! Be Little Chirakarin today! Are you taking a long time in coming to greet me here because of some regret? Have you been delayed by sleeping for a long time, Little Chirakarin, or because you are concerned about the long-lasting anguish of both of us?'

The great sage Gautama lamented like this, and then he saw his son Chirakarin standing near him, holding the knife with which he was to have killed his mother. When Chirakarin saw his father, he became extremely unhappy. Throwing away his knife, he asked for pardon, bowing his head. But when Gautama saw his son fallen on the ground, touching it with his head, and when he saw his wife there in her usual form, he was filled with great joy. His son stood there, hoping not to be blamed for his failure to kill, humbly asking to be forgiven for what he had (not) done. When the father saw his son bowing low at his feet, he realized that his son's dithering about using the weapon had saved him from danger. The father praised his son for a long time [*chira*], smelling him on the head in affection for a long time, and embracing him with his two arms for a long time, and saying, 'May you live for a long time!'

And so the wise Gautama, filled with love and joy, congratulated his son: 'Thank you for taking a long time! Go on taking a long time for a long time! While you were taking a long time, I was miserable for a long time.' And Gautama, whose *tapas* was very great, spent many years—a long time—in that ashram and then went to heaven together with his son.

[12.258]

8. How Sudarshana, the Son of Fire, Let His Wife Sleep with Dharma

Class and money are, once again, at issue in this story about a marriage, for Fire (Agni), the incarnation of the sacrificial fire, here takes the form of a poor Brahmin, and his desire for a human princess of a royal line—indeed, the daughter of King Duryodhana, the arch enemy of King Yudhishthira to whom the story is told—is, as so often, problematic. But the story has a happy ending, for the heroine is a good, virtuous wife, who eventually becomes the Oghavati River. The main purpose of the story is to explain how even a householder—who does not have access to the sorts of power achieved by a man of *tapas*, or by a man who renounces the comforts of married life—can still fulfil his own dharma, the dharma of a householder, in such a way as to go to heaven, especially if he has a truly obedient wife.

The Text

Yudhishthira asked Bhishma if any householder was ever able to conquer death by following the dharma of a householder. Bhishma replied, 'They do tell an ancient story about this, about a householder who conquered death by following his dharma.' He began by tracing the lineage of the daughter of King Duryodhana, and then he continued:

The god of Fire desired the daughter of King Duryodhana. Taking on the visible form of a Brahmin, he asked King Duryodhana for his daughter. The king thought, 'This man is poor, and not of the same class as I am,' and he did not wish to give his daughter to the Brahmin. But when Duryodhana was giving a sacrifice, Fire, who carries the oblation, disappeared from the sacrifice. Then King Duryodhana said to his sacrificial priests, 'What evil deed could I have done, or you have done, which caused Fire to disappear as if evil people had done something? For it could be no small misdeed on our part to make Fire disappear. You did it or I did it. Think about this truly.' When they heard what the king said, the Brahmins held their tongues and sought refuge with Fire. Fire revealed to them his own blazing form, shining like the sun in autumn, and said to the Brahmins, 'I have asked for Duryodhana's daughter to be mine.'

Then all the Brahmins, astonished, stood up promptly and reported to the king what Fire had said. The intelligent king rejoiced greatly and said 'Yes!' to Fire's request. And the bride price that he asked Fire for was: 'Be always near me here, Fire.' And Fire replied to the king, 'So be it.'

King Duryodhana had his daughter adorned in new garments and gave her to Fire, who received the princess with the Vedic rites just as he receives the drops of butter in the sacrifice. Enchanted by her beauty, nature, noble lineage, shape, and grace, Fire made her pregnant. A son was born in her, the son of Fire, named Sudarshana. Even as a child, Sudarshana studied the entire Veda; and he grew to manhood.

There was a king named Oghavan, who had a divinely beautiful daughter named Oghavati, whom he gave to the wise Sudarshana, son of Fire, to be his wife. Sudarshana took great delight in living as a householder with Oghavati. He made a vow: 'Living as a householder, I will conquer death!' And he said to Oghavati, 'You must never ever do anything in opposition to a guest. Whatever you can do to satisfy the guest, always, without exception, even if it means giving yourself, you who have such beautiful loins, you should not hesitate to do it. This vow is always in my heart, for there is nothing more important than a guest for those who are householders. If you—who have such beautiful thighs and are so lovely—accept my words as your authority, keep these words in your heart always. You must never refuse a guest anything, whether I have gone out, my flawless beauty, or am here.' Oghavati raised her cupped hands to her head and said, 'I will never in any way fail to do anything that you have told me to do.'

But Death, knowing that Sudarshana was trying to conquer death in this way, kept following behind him, constantly searching for a chink in his moral armour. One day when Sudarshana had gone out to get firewood, a handsome Brahmin came there as a guest and said to Oghavati, 'How lovely you are! I want you to grant me the privileges of a guest today, as a test of your dharma as a householder.' The beautiful princess, hearing this from the

Brahmin, received him with the rituals enjoined by the Veda. She offered the Brahmin guest a seat, and water to wash his feet, and said to him, 'What is your purpose here, and what can I give you?'

The Brahmin then replied to the princess Oghavati, 'I have come here for you, you lovely creature, so do what I want, without hesitating. If your dharma as a householder is put to this test, princess, you ought to do what I want by giving yourself to me.' The princess offered him other desirable things, but the Brahmin chose no boon other than that she must give herself to him. And so the princess, remembering every word of her husband's speech, said, 'Yes,' to that bull of a Brahmin, though she was ashamed. She and the Brahmin lay down together intimately, as she remembered the words of her husband who so longed to follow the rules of the life of a householder.

Now, when Sudarshana had gathered up the firewood, he returned, still constantly followed by Death as if he were a close friend. When Sudarshana came to the ashram, he called out for Oghavati, 'Where have you gone?' again and again. She gave no reply to her husband, for, though she was true to her husband, she was in the arms of the Brahmin. 'I have been defiled,' she thought, and was ashamed before her husband. And so the good woman remained silent and didn't say anything at all. Sudarshana called out to her once again and worried: 'Where can that good woman be? Where has she gone? What can be more important to her than me? She always kept her vows to her husband, was always true and virtuous, always taking pleasure in propriety. How then is it that she doesn't come back to meet me today, smiling, just as she used to do in the past?'

The Brahmin inside the house replied to Sudarshana: 'Son of Fire, know that I, a Brahmin, have arrived as a guest. Your wife, who is lovely to look at, gratified me with various services for a guest, her mind firmly set on propriety. She honoured me with this activity. Good sir, you should say what is appropriate here and now.' Death, with his hammer in his hand ready to respond, thought, 'As soon as he has broken his vow, I will kill him.'

But Sudarshana had conquered his anger and renounced all vengeance, in his mind, action, sight and speech, and so he smiled and said, 'Best of Brahmins, I hope you have enjoyed the sex; that would give me great pleasure. For the primary dharma for a householder is to honour any guest that arrives. Wise men say that there is no other dharma higher than that of a householder whose guest departs well honoured. I have taken a vow to give to guests my life's breaths and my wife, and any other treasure that I may have. As what I have said today is not false, by that truth may the gods protect me.'

Then a great sound arose in all the quarters of the sky, over and over again, everywhere, saying, 'It is true! It is not false!' And then the Brahmin came out from the hut, rising up like the wind, filling the earth and the sky with his own form. Making the three worlds resound with his refined voice, he spoke to Sudarshana, the man who knew dharma, first introducing himself by his name: 'I am Dharma. I came here to test you, and as I know your truth, I am extremely pleased with you. You have conquered Death here, who has been following you, always searching for a vulnerable place in you, but you overcame him through your fortitude. And no one in the triple world has the power even to look upon this virtuous wife of yours, firm in her vow to her husband. She is protected by your virtues and by the virtues of a woman who keeps her vows to her husband. She cannot be raped, and whatever she says cannot be otherwise. For she is girded by her own *tapas*, and she speaks the truth.

'In order to purify the world, one half of this gifted woman will become a supreme river, the Oghavati, and the other half, her body, will follow you. With her you will go to the worlds that you have won by your *tapas*, eternal and perpetual worlds, from whence there is no return. And you will have these worlds in this very body, for you have conquered death.'

For a householder, there is no divinity but the guest. A householder who does not honour a virtuous guest gives his good karma to the guest and dies in dishonour. This is the best story about a householder who, once upon a time, conquered death.

[13.2]

9. How Jamadagni Protected his Wife Renuka from the Sun

We have briefly considered the birth and lineage of Jamadagni, the peculiarities of which (due to his mother's failure to conceive him properly[17]) explain, at least in part, his notoriously bad temper. At the start of this next story, Jamadagni treats his wife, Renuka, thoughtlessly and insultingly, though not cruelly. Yet his relationship with Renuka is sometimes much nastier than this: in a much-retold tale, when she has what he regards as an unchaste thought, he orders their son Parashu Rama to kill her, and he does. Jamadagni is much nicer to her in this story, just as Ahalya's husband Gautama is much nicer than usual to her in the story of the Procrastinator. And Renuka is here portrayed as a model wife, who does not complain about being treated thoughtlessly until she is in serious pain. Yet even here, though she is the one who has suffered from the heat, in the end it is to him, and not to her, that the sun, the god Surya, gives the gifts that protect mortals from the sun.

The Text

Yudhishthira said, 'At the celebrations for the ancestors, and on other auspicious occasions, too, they give an umbrella and a pair of sandals. Who started this? How did the custom arise, and why are these things given?' Bhishma said, 'Listen attentively and I will tell you about umbrellas and sandals in detail, about how this practice began in the world. Listen to this story about a conversation between Jamadagni and the Sun that took place in the old times.'

Once upon a time, Jamadagni used to play at archery, placing his arrows one by one and shooting them. He took pleasure in the sounds of the bow string and the arrow. His wife Renuka would gather up all the arrows he had shot and give them to him, again and again; he would shoot them and she would return them.

One day when the sun had climbed to midday at the beginning of the month of May [Jyeshtha], Jamadagni shot his arrows and said to Renuka, 'Go and fetch these arrows I shot from my bow, so that I can shoot them again.' But she went into the shade of a tree and stayed there, for her head and her feet were very hot; she was perspiring, and her feet hurt. She stayed there just for a moment, in pain, but she was afraid her husband would curse her, and so she went to bring the arrows back to him. Then she went up to her husband, trembling in fear of him. The sage was angry and said to her, 'Renuka, why have you taken such a long time to come back again?' Renuka said, 'My head is burning, and my feet, too. I am tormented by the energy of the sun, and so I sought refuge in the shade of a tree. That is why I took such a long time. Now that you know this, do not be angry with me.'

Jamadagni said, 'Today I will use my arrows, that are full of the energy of fire, to shoot down this sun whose blazing rays are giving you such pain.' He drew his divine bow and took up many arrows and stood facing the sun. As he was about to strike, the sun, Surya, came to him in the form of a Brahmin and said, 'What has the sun done to offend you? The sun with his rays takes juices up into the sky from here and there and then rains down the liquid in the form of rains. Food grows from that, making humans prosper. "Food is the breath of life," it is said in the Vedas. Hidden in the clouds, surrounded by his rays, the sun sends rain down upon the several continents. You know all this that I have just been saying. Calm down. Why are you trying to bring down the sun?'

Jamadagni laughed out loud and said to the sun, 'Surya, do not fear, since you have sought my protection. Think of a way that a path heated by your rays can still be made comfortable.' Surya quickly gave him an umbrella and sandals and said: 'Please accept this umbrella to protect your head and fend off my rays, and this pair of leather sandals to protect your feet. And from today forth, in this world, among all the auspicious gifts, these will always be the best.'

[13.97–98]

10. How Utathya Got his Wife Back from Varuna

The wife in this story (who is the daughter of Soma, the incarnation of the sacred plant whose juice intoxicates the gods) has no voice at all. She is just a pawn that the men fight over, though she may be guilty of not resisting the sexual attentions of the god Varuna when he carries her off.

The Text

Yudhishthira asked Bhishma about the benefits of honouring Brahmins. Bhishma told him several stories, including this one:

Soma had a very beautiful daughter named Bhadra, and he thought that the Brahmin Utathya would be a good husband for her, her equal. Bhadra chose Utathya for her husband, and Soma summoned Utathya and gave his glorious daughter to him; Utathya received her for his wife with all the rituals.

But some time before this, Varuna, god of the waters, had desired Bhadra, and now he came to Utathya's forest ashram on the Yamuna River and took her away to his own city, a place of great marvels, with six hundred thousand lakes and palaces and Apsarases and divine pleasures. And there the god Varuna enjoyed her.

The sage Narada reported to Utathya that his wife was being oppressed. Then Utathya said to Narada, 'Go to Varuna and speak harshly to him, telling him from me, "Release my wife. Why did you take her away? You are one of the gods who protect people; you aren't supposed to ravish them. Soma gave my wife to me, but you took her away."' Narada said to Varuna, 'Release Utathya's wife.' But Varuna replied, 'This woman is very dear to me, and I cannot bear to give her up.' Narada was not very happy to hear this, but he went back to Utathya and said, 'Varuna grabbed me by the throat and threw me out. He did not give back your wife. Do what you must do.' At this, Utathya blazed up in anger, and with his fiery energy and great *tapas* he paralysed the waters and drank them up. This destroyed Varuna's allies, but still Varuna did not give up Utathya's wife.

Then Utathya, in a fury, said to the earth, 'Show me dry land, in place of your six hundred thousand lakes.' And so a desert arose, and the ocean drained away from that place. And Utathya said to the river Sarasvati, 'Go to the desert and vanish!' When that area had been dried up to powder, Varuna took Utathya's wife to safety and gave her to Utathya, who rejoiced to receive his wife. Utathya released Varuna from his misery and then he took his wife and went home.

[13.139]

11. How Durvasas Tormented and Rewarded Krishna and Rukmini

This story is told in the first-person by the person who experienced it—Krishna, who tells it to Pradyumna, his son born to his wife Rukmini (chief among his 16,000 wives). It is a strange variant of an important Indo-European myth, the Indian equivalent of Achilles' heel (and Siegfried's shoulder), explaining why Krishna was invulnerable except on the bottoms of his feet, which is indeed where an archer ultimately shoots him and kills him. (16.5.16–21[18]) The substance that would make Krishna immortal is a magic form of *payasa*, a kind of rice-pudding, made of milk, rice and sugar.

That part of the story is well known, but this text idiosyncratically adds another incident involving the gratuitous torture of a woman, Rukmini. For, in the course of urging that even particularly nasty Brahmins be tolerated, the text praises a woman who undergoes painful and insulting treatment at the hands of a notoriously horrid Brahmin, Durvasas (whose name significantly means 'Badly Housed' or, perhaps better, 'Hard to House'). And the woman's husband, Krishna, tells this brutal story to their son.

The Text

Pradyumna asked his father, Krishna, 'What is the reward for honouring Brahmins?' And Krishna told him this story in reply.

A Brahmin named Durvasas lived in my house. He was tawny and yellow, wore a bark garment, and his beard and nails were long. He was taller than the tallest man on earth. He moved around the worlds of gods and men, singing these songs in public squares and assemblies: 'Who will house the Brahmin Durvasas and honour him in his home? Hearing my words, who will give me shelter? And who will house me and not get angry with me?' Since no one invited him, I housed him. On one day, he would eat food that would have fed many thousands. And on another day, he ate very little or did not return to the house. He would laugh for no reason and then weep for no reason, and there was then on earth no one his equal in vigour. He went into our living quarters and burnt the beds, the coverings, and the clothes of the well-dressed maidens, and then he went out.

Then Durvasas said to me, 'Krishna, I wish to eat some *payasa*. Right away.' I had always known what he was thinking and so I had already told the servants in the house to have *all* food and drink and edibles on hand, and I had already, earlier, urged them, 'Let all the rituals of hospitality take place.' And so I presented him with hot *payasa*, and he ate it fast and then said, 'Quickly, smear your limbs with *payasa*.' Without hesitating, I did just that: I smeared my limbs and my head with his leftovers.

Then he saw your beautiful young mother, Rukmini, near him and, smiling, he had her, too, smeared with the *payasa*.

Then the sage quickly yoked her—with all her limbs smeared with *payasa*—to his chariot and mounted the chariot. He was sitting on the axle of the chariot, and as I was looking on, he struck Rukmini with the goad. But I had not even a spark of the misery brought on by possessiveness and pride, and so I did and said nothing, and he went out on the great royal road. When the people of my family saw this great marvel, they were full of righteous anger, and some of them muttered to one another about it, saying, 'Let only Brahmins, and no other class whatever, be born, for what other man here could mount this chariot and live? The venom from a serpent's poisonous fang is sharp, but the poisonous venom of a Brahmin is sharper, for there is no cure for one who has been burnt by the venom of a Brahmin.'

When Durvasas went on, Rukmini stumbled on the path. He had no patience with her, but quickly whipped her. Then, in a high fury, he jumped down from the chariot and ran on foot along the wrong path, heading South. Still smeared with the *payasa*, I ran after him as he was running on the wrong path; I kept saying 'Sir, have mercy!' Then he looked back and said to me, 'Krishna, you have conquered your anger. I have seen no offence in you in this matter. I am pleased with you. Choose any boons that you desire. See the sort of reward that I can grant when I am pleased: people will be as attached to you as they are to their food; you will be beloved by all people. Whatever of yours has been broken or burnt or in any way destroyed, you will see all of that just as it was, or better. And wherever this *payasa* has been smeared on your limbs, you will have no danger of death as long as you wish. But why did you not smear the soles of your feet today? That does not please me.' I looked at my own body and saw that it had become glorious.

Then, pleased, he said to Rukmini, 'You will have the glory of being the best of all women, and your fame in the world will be unparalleled. Neither old age nor illness nor pallor will touch you, and you will have a sweet smell and will delight Krishna. Of the sixteen thousand wives of Krishna, you will be the best, and will share his ultimate world.' When he had said this to your mother, Durvasas spoke again to me as he set out, blazing like a fire: 'May your attitude to Brahmins always be like this!' And then he vanished, and I made this private vow: 'Whatever a Brahmin says, I will do it all.' Then I entered the house with your mother, rejoicing in my soul, and I saw that everything was made new, whatever the Brahmin had broken or burnt. I was amazed to see that everything was new and solid, and in my mind I honoured that Brahmin.

[13.144]

12. How Narada Married Srinjaya's Daughter

Despite his conversation with Panchachuda[19] and his full awareness of the wickedness of women, the divine sage Narada himself falls victim to their charms. And the woman with whom he falls in love, King Srinjaya's daughter Sukumari, is a paradigm of wifely virtue: though she thinks her husband is a monkey, she is faithful to him. But does he stay with her? At the end of this adventure, Narada is said to go 'back home'. This might mean that Narada went back to his conjugal life with Sukumari, but, given Narada's track record and the fact that we hear no more about Sukumari, I think it is more likely that he went back to his usual life as a wandering celibate sage on earth or, indeed, back to heaven—in either case, deserting her.

The Text

Yudhishthira asked Krishna, 'How did Narada marry King Srinjaya's daughter?' Krishna replied, 'I will tell you right now what happened.'

Long ago, Narada and Parvata were sages that all the people honoured. Narada was Parvata's maternal uncle; Parvata was his nephew, the son of Narada's sister. One day, the two of them came here from the world of the gods, wishing to enjoy themselves, to take their pleasures among humans.

They were powerful through their *tapas*, and their food was the purifying sacrificial oblation. But the two of them, wandering on the surface of the earth, ran around and enjoyed human pleasures and human food. Full of affection, full of pleasure, the two great sages made an agreement: 'Whoever gets an idea or a wish in his heart, whether good or bad, he must report it to the other. If he lies, he will be cursed.'

Then they went to King Srinjaya and said, 'We two will live with you for a while. Treat us well, and it will be for your benefit.' 'Yes!' said the king, and he received them with due honours. Then, one day, when the king had grown very fond of the two of them, he said to them, 'This is my only daughter, who will serve the two of you. She is as beautiful, with her faultless limbs, as she is virtuous, a young girl delicate as a lotus filament. Her name is Sukumari.' 'Very well, sir,' they said, and the king then instructed her: 'My daughter, serve these two Brahmins as if they were gods, or your ancestors.' 'So be it,' said the virtuous maiden to her father, and she served the two sages just as the king had commanded.

But because of the way she served them, and because of her incomparable beauty, desire swiftly and violently overcame Narada. And that lust grew in his heart just as the moon steadily waxes during the bright half of the month. He was so ashamed that he did not tell his noble nephew Parvata about his intense desire. But Parvata, through his own *tapas* and through Narada's unconscious signs and revealing movements, realized that Narada was overcome by desire, and in anger he cursed him very severely: 'You made an agreement with me in cold blood, that whatever desire, good or bad, arose in the heart of either of us, we would tell one another. And now you have made those words false. So this is what I say to you: Since you did not speak to me about this desire that you felt for Sukumari, I curse you. Since, though you are my senior, and you know the Vedas and practice *tapas* and are a Brahmin, you broke the mutual agreement that the two of us had made, I curse you: Sukumari will be your wife, there is no doubt, but from the moment of the marriage, she will see you as a monkey, and other people, too, will see you in that form and not in your own shape.'

When Narada understood these words from Parvata, in fury he cursed him in return, the uncle cursing his nephew: 'Even though you have achieved *tapas* and chastity and truth and self-control, and are constantly ruled by dharma, you will never live in heaven.' And so the two of them, unable to endure one another, rushed together like a pair of raging bull elephants and gave one another terrible curses.

Then the great sage Parvata wandered over the whole earth and was honoured properly because of his glory. And Narada married Srinjaya's daughter Sukumari, in accordance with dharma. But because of the curse, from the moment the priest pronounced the mantras and joined their hands, Sukumari saw Narada as a monkey. Yet she did not treat him with contempt but was always affectionate to him. She went to her husband's bed and did not even think of going to any other man, or to any god or sage. She was faithful to her husband.

Then one day Parvata was walking about in a deserted forest and saw Narada there. Greeting Narada, Parvata approached him respectfully and cupped his hands in reverence and said, 'Do me a favour, my lord, and let me go to heaven.' Narada saw how miserable Parvata was, and as Narada himself was even more miserable, he said, 'You were the one who cursed me first, saying, "You will be a monkey." Since you were like a son to me, this was not seemly of you. And only after you had said this to me did I, afterwards, curse you, too, in revenge, saying, "From this very day, you will never be able to dwell in heaven."' And so the two sages withdrew their curses from one another.

When Sukumari then saw Narada in his glorious godlike form, she thought he must be someone else's husband, and she ran away. But when Parvata saw her running away, for which she could not be blamed, he said, 'This is your husband; do not worry about that. This is your lord and master, the great sage Narada. His heart belongs only to you.' Parvata continued to persuade her in various ways, and when she heard that her husband had suffered from a curse, she regained her normal disposition. Parvata then went to heaven and Narada went back home.

[12.30]

II. Stories about Fathers and Sons

The *Mahabharata* abounds in stories about fathers mourning for their dead sons, part of the more general lamentation for the dead that is a central leitmotif of Bhishma's sermons to Yudhishthira. There are few stories about sons who mourn their fathers, perhaps because this is regarded as part of the normal course of life. But there are stories about sons who are better than their fathers, a more cheerful, but also more problematic, line of thought.

The sons have special properties that make them better than their fathers. Srinjaya's son is named Suvarnashtivin, which literally means 'Gold-excreting', an ability that the people in the story regard as a great gift, though this text never describes the uses of this ability. The theme of a child who produces gold, sometimes from the mouth and sometimes from the anus, recurs in European literature, in some of the tales of the brothers Grimm; Freud wrote about the recurrent connections between gold and faeces. But Srinjaya's special powers play no part in this story; what matters is that he becomes a great king and rules well for many years, which is all that any king—such as, to take a case at random, Yudhishthira—could hope for in a son.

Vyasa's son Shuka is the direct product of Vyasa's uncontrolled sexual passion, but Shuka himself is entirely free of passion. Where Vyasa disturbs the Apsarases who are bathing naked, making them run away and cover their bodies, they do nothing at all when Shuka comes near them, for they know that he has transcended all passions. When Vyasa realizes that his son has achieved what he himself can never achieve, he is said to be both 'pleased and ashamed', a wonderful expression of the ambivalence of a father towards a son whom he knows to have excelled him. And Vyasa is finally given a boon that represents the impossible dream and hope of most devoted fathers: that he would see, always and everywhere, the image of his son.

13. How Narada Revived King Srinjaya's Son

On one occasion when Yudhishthira was grieving over the deaths of his kin, Krishna told him, to cheer him up, a series of tales of fathers who grieved over the deaths of their sons. Among these stories, Krishna told Yudhishthira how, in order to console King Srinjaya after the death of his son, Narada had told him a series of stories about great kings whose sons—greater than the ones that Yudhishthira and Srinjaya were mourning—died. (12.29) In this final episode of that series, King Srinjaya's son dies but comes back to life, the happiest of all happy endings.

We have heard the story of Narada's marriage to Srinjaya's daughter. In this sequel to that story, Srinjaya's daughter is never mentioned, but Srinjaya's son Suvarnashtivin dies and is revived. Krishna introduces the story, as he introduced the story of Narada's marriage, but now Narada himself tells the story.

The Text

Yudhishthira asked Krishna, 'How was King Srinjaya's son born?' Krishna replied, 'The great sage Narada saw all this with his own eyes. He will tell you everything that happened if you ask him.' Narada said:

Parvata was my sister's son. He and I went to King Srinjaya, who honoured us in every way and gave us everything we wanted. When many years had passed, and it was time to go, Parvata said to me, 'We two have lived in the house of this king and have been treated with great honour. We must now think about what is proper for the present moment.' I replied to Parvata, 'Let us make the king happy by granting him a boon. Let him have whatever he wishes.' We summoned King Srinjaya and offered him a boon: 'Accept from us whatever does not cause harm to the gods but is useful for humans.'

Srinjaya said, 'I want a heroic son, one who is courageous and holds fast to his vows, who will have a long life and good luck, and who will be as glorious as Indra the king of the gods.' Parvata said, 'You will get your wish, but he will not have a long life, since in your heart you wanted to surpass Indra the king of the gods. Your son will be called Suvarnashthivin ['Gold-excreting'], because he will excrete gold. He will be as glorious as Indra, but he must be protected from Indra.'

When Srinjaya heard what Parvata had said, he pleaded with him, saying, 'Don't let this happen! By the power of your *tapas*, great sage, let my son have a long life!' Parvata said nothing to him, because he was worried about Indra. But I spoke again to the miserable king: 'Whenever you think of me, your majesty, I will appear to you. And when your beloved son has fallen into the power of the king of the dead, I will give him back to you in his own body. Do not grieve, your majesty.' And we two set out for where we wanted to go, and Srinjaya went back into his palace.

At a certain moment in the twisting of Time, a son was born to Srinjaya, manly and blazing with energy. In time, he grew up and became 'Gold-excreting', both in name and in deed. This most amazing fact spread throughout the world, and Indra the king of the gods learned of the boon that Narada and Parvata had given to Srinjaya. Afraid that he might be overpowered by this boy, Indra sought for a weakness in him. He commanded the embodied form of his divine weapon, the thunderbolt: 'Become a tiger and kill the king's son. If this son that Parvata gave to Srinjaya grows up, he will surpass me in manliness.' The thunderbolt took the form of a tiger and constantly followed the boy around, looking for an opening. As for Srinjaya, now that he had a son as glorious as Indra, he was thrilled and spent all his time in the forest with the boy among the women of the inner citadel, the harem.

One day, the boy was running about playing at a forest waterfall on the banks of the Ganges, and his nurse was the only one with him. He was now five years old, but as brave as a bull elephant, and he had great strength. Suddenly he came upon a tiger, who sprang at him. The tiger mauled the trembling prince, who fell lifeless to the ground. The nurse screamed in her great agony. Then the tiger vanished right there, through the magic of Indra. When King Srinjaya heard the nurse's screams and sobs, he ran to that place. He saw the boy lying there lifeless, drenched in blood, his chest crushed in. He took his son on his lap and wept in his agony. The boy's mothers, weeping and devastated by sorrow, ran to King Srinjaya.

Then the king, who had forgotten me, now remembered me. And as soon as I knew that he had thought of me, I made myself visible to him. Since he was besotted with grief, I told Srinjaya what Krishna had told you, Yudhishthira, about the deaths of sons, and then I revived the boy, with Indra's permission. What was fated to be that way could not be otherwise. And so the heroic young man, famed as 'Gold-excreting', delighted the hearts of his father and mother. And when his father had gone to heaven, Suvarnashtivin ruled the kingdom for a thousand and a hundred years. His prowess was great, and he performed many sacrifices with many generous donations to the priests, satisfying the gods and his ancestors. He begat many sons to continue the lineage, and after a long time he succumbed to the dharma of Time.

[12.31]

14. How Vyasa's Son Shuka Was Born

Two stories tell about the birth of Shuka and his relationship with his father, Vyasa. Now, Vyasa is a great Brahmin sage, the author (and sometimes the narrator) of the *Mahabharata*, but he is also bound to the world by his involvement in the plot of his own text. For Vyasa is the grandfather of the Pandavas, of whom the eldest is Yudhishthira, to whom these stories are being told. Vyasa's relationship with his son, Shuka, involves some of the problems that other fathers (and gurus) have with their sons (and disciples). For the gods, too, and supernatural sages like Vyasa, have problem children, differently problematic from the children of mere mortals.

'Shuka' means 'parrot', and so the story tells us that Shuka's mother took the form of a parrot. And her name includes the word for 'butter', as Vyasa's semen falls into the fire just like the butter that is used in a sacrifice.

The Text

Yudhishthira asked, 'How was Shuka born to Vyasa? In what woman did Vyasa beget Shuka? For we know nothing about his mother or his birth.' Bhishma replied:

Vyasa generated *tapas* for many years with great devotion, and pleased Shiva so well that Shiva decided to grant Vyasa what he wanted. And so Shiva, smiling, said to Vyasa, 'Your son will be just as you wish him to be. Your son will be like fire, like wind, like earth, like water, pure as the sky. His intelligence will be great, and he will achieve great fame.'

When Vyasa had obtained this great boon from the god, he churned the firestick to make a fire. Just then the sage saw a supremely beautiful Apsaras named Ghritachi ['Shining with Butter']. When Vyasa saw the Apsaras, he was suddenly deluded by desire, his mind agitated by passion. She then became a female parrot and went to him. He saw that the Apsaras had been concealed in another form, but his desire was relentless and pervaded all his limbs. He gripped the desire in his heart with great fortitude, but he was not able to contain his mind as it escaped in all directions, nor to control his emotions, and he was bewitched by Ghritachi's body. As the sage made a great effort to control himself, while he still wanted to make a fire, suddenly his semen fell right on his firestick. With an unhesitating mind, despite everything, Vyasa churned the firestick, and Shuka ['the parrot'] was born out of the womb of the firestick. Just as, in a sacrifice, the kindled fire blazes when it has received the oblation of butter, in the very same way Shuka blazed with his energy when he was born. He had his father's superb form and colouring, shining like a smokeless fire.

[12.310–311]

15. How Shuka Surpassed Vyasa

We have seen that the birth of Shuka was due to his father's vulnerability to women. The son, however, does not inherit his father's weakness.

The Text

Yudhishthira said, 'Tell me about Shuka's greatness, and about his wisdom.' Bhishma said:

The gods and Gandharvas and sages and Yakshas and Rakshasas all honoured Shuka. When he came down from heaven on his final journey, the air was filled with divine flowers everywhere. Then, from above, Shuka saw the heavenly form of the river Ganges, lined by its forests of flowering trees. Troops of Apsarases were bathing and playing in that river. When they saw Shuka, they took no notice of him, even though they were not wearing any garments, for his form was empty.

When Vyasa learned that his son Shuka was moving on in this way on the ultimate journey, he was filled with affection for him and followed behind. Shuka was going through the air on a path above the winds, demonstrating his great powers. Vyasa, using his *tapas*, engaged in the supreme path of yoga and in the blink of an eye went to the place where Shuka had alighted. He saw a mountain peak that Shuka had split in two, and the sages there praised his son's deeds to him. He shouted, 'Shuka!' for a long time, loudly, making the three worlds resound with his voice. But Shuka had become dissolved into the universe, and so he responded with the echoing sound of 'Ho!' Then the whole universe, moving and still, sent back loudly the sound of the single syllable 'Ho!' And from that time forward, even today, when individual sounds are uttered loudly, in mountains and caves and canyons, they echo, as if answering Shuka, 'Ho!'

Shuka vanished and achieved his supreme final destination.

But when Vyasa saw the greatness of his son, he sat down on the slope of the mountain, thinking about him. Now, when the troops of Apsarases who were playing on the banks of the heavenly Ganges saw the sage, they all became frightened and confused. Some plunged into the water, and some ran into the bushes; some put on their clothes. Vyasa then realized that his son had attained freedom from rebirth, while he himself was still attached. And he became both pleased and ashamed.

Shiva came to Vyasa, surrounded by the gods and Gandharvas and the troops of great sages, and spoke to him, beginning with words of comfort, knowing that Vyasa was deeply distressed by his grief for his son. Shiva said, 'In the past, you asked me for a son who would be, in his valour, like Fire, Earth, the Waters, the Wind and the Air. And because of your *tapas*, and through my power, such a son was born to you, glorious and pure. He has gone to the finest final destination, hard to obtain even by those who have conquered their senses, even by the gods. So why are you grieving for him? As long as the mountains stand, as long as the oceans remain, for so long will the undying fame of your son go on. And, by my grace, in this world you will see a shadow image just like your son, everywhere, never disappearing.' And just as Shiva had told him, the sage Vyasa saw the shadow image and turned back, rejoicing greatly.

[12.320]

III. Stories about Animals

Most of the stories about animals in this text, like most animal fables throughout the world (think 'Aesop' or, in India, 'Jatakas'), are not really about animals at all, but just use animals as stereotypes of certain sorts of human beings.

Jackals are generally dishonest and disgusting, greedy and unclean (eaters of carrion), but in one of our stories ('How the Tiger's Mother Saved the Pious Jackal'), the jackal is the hero, honest and pious; he even fasts to death at the end. And the tiger, generally regarded in India as the king of beasts (a title that other folklores, particularly in Africa, usually award to the lion), in that story is an easily duped fool, who—in a rare feminist moment in this collection of stories—is saved from his stupidity and ingratitude by the intervention of his wise mother. But in the very next story ('How the Jackal Ate the Lazy Camel'), the jackal reverts to type; all he cares about is eating another animal.

Many of the stories are about politics (*artha*, in the Indian scheme of the three goals of life), and the policies they cite are recommended by the *Arthashastra*, a cynical and pitiless ancient Sanskrit text on political science attributed to Brihaspati, the consigliere of the gods, who makes Machiavelli look like St Francis.

16. How the Tiger's Mother Saved the Pious Jackal

This object lesson in hypocrisy features a jackal (a notoriously unclean, cowardly and despicable carrion-eating animal) who in this case is a moral hero. There is also a rare cameo appearance of a virtuous tiger who is also a virtuous female. The story is unusual in its argument that an animal (and perhaps, by extension, a human) can reject the low habits of the species or caste into which he is born and achieve a higher and more virtuous status.

The Text

Yudhishthira said, 'There are people who are unpleasant but seem pleasant; and there are people who are pleasant but look unpleasant. How can we know such men?' Bhishma said, 'On this subject they tell this ancient story about a conversation between a tiger and a jackal. Learn from it.'

Once upon a time, in a prosperous city, there was a king who was the worst sort of man, a cruel man who took pleasure in hurting other people. And so, when his lifespan ran out, he underwent a most undesirable rebirth: defiled by his previous karma, he became a jackal. But he remembered his previous birth and so became indifferent to worldly objects. Committed to non-injury towards all creatures, speaking the truth, firm in keeping his vows, by his own preference he did not eat meat, even when others got it for him; he ate nothing but fruits that had fallen from the trees.

This jackal still chose to live in a cremation ground, because of his affection for it as the place of his birth, and no other dwelling pleased him. The other jackals of his line could not bear his purity; they tried to change his mind by saying to him, respectfully but frankly: 'Though you live in this horrible forest of our ancestors, you want to maintain purity. This is perverse in you, since you are a flesh-eater. But be like us, and we will provide you with food. Give up purity and eat, for whatever you eat is your food.'

The jackal replied, calmly, with honeyed words that were courteous, reasonable, and not harsh: 'I do not regard my birth as the only criterion. Conduct is what determines lineage. I wish to do what will make me famous far and wide. Even if I live in a cremation ground, my meditation will cancel that out. The ashram is no indication of dharma. A person who lives in an ashram might kill a Brahmin, but someone who is not in an ashram might make the gift of a cow. Is killing a Brahmin not a sin that will cause one to fall to hell? Or will the gift of the cow, on the other hand, be in vain? Because of your consuming greed, you take pleasure in nothing but eating. And because you are confused, you do not see the faults in that attachment. I scorn this behaviour, for it is disgusting, inspires distrust, distracts one from the proper goals, and is harmful in this world and the next.'

A tiger, king of beasts, famous for his courage, regarded the jackal as pure and learned. The tiger treated the jackal with the same honour that he himself received, and he wanted to elevate the jackal to make him his minister. But the jackal replied, 'I am satisfied with what I have; working for hire would make me miserable. I know nothing about service, as I just live in the forest, doing whatever I want. Those who live by serving the king provoke his censure when they make mistakes. But life in the forest is without any attachments, without danger, without restraints or impediments. Fear takes hold in the heart of someone who is summoned by a king, but not in people who are satisfied by living in the forest, eating fruits and roots. Food and water are easy to get here, but risky there. Some servants are disciplined by kings because they have made mistakes; but just as many are destroyed because they have been calumniated by people whom they have offended. Considering all this, I see that happiness is found where there is no attachment.

'But if the king of beasts thinks that I should do this, I wish to have an agreement made about how I am to be treated. You must honour my opinions and listen to what I say for your own good. And you must adhere firmly to the treatment that you devise for me. I will not confer about anything with your other advisors; they are politically savvy and, wishing to protect themselves, they will speak falsely about me. Meeting with you in secret, each of us alone, I will tell you what is good for you. But you must not question me about what is beneficial or harmful in matters that concern the affairs of your relatives. When you have consulted me, you must not afterwards do anything harmful to your other advisors. And if you become angry with my people, you must not punish them.' The tiger said, 'So be it,' and so the jackal became the advisor on policy for the tiger in his lair.

Seeing that the jackal was so honoured in this way, and so engaged in his tasks, the former ministers hated him and banded together against him. Conciliating the jackal with the pretence of friendship, and trying to bring him into their camp, these vicious-minded creatures wanted to win the jackal over to their evil ways. In the past, when matters were different, they had been accustomed to stealing other peoples' valuables; but now, under the jackal's control, they were not able to get any precious things at all. They tempted him with stories, hoping to get him to swerve from his proper path; and they enticed him with large sums of money. But he was so intelligent that he did not waver from his constancy. And so those others planned to destroy him.

The tiger king liked meat that had been well prepared. They stole his meat and put it in the jackal's house. The jackal knew all about it—why it had been stolen, and by whom, and as part of what plan—but he endured it patiently, for a good reason: When he had agreed to become the king's minister, he had demanded this promise: 'If you wish to remain my friend, you must never take offence with me.' Now, when the tiger's meal was placed before him, and the meat was not there, the tiger commanded: 'Hunt for the thief!' But the liars said, 'It was stolen by your learned minister, who thinks he's so smart.' When he heard of the jackal's disloyalty, the tiger king became furious and indignant, and he wanted to have him killed.

The former advisors, seeing their opening, said, 'He is working to shatter all of our livelihoods. When he does something like this, he is protected by your affection. But he is not really the sort of person your majesty heard that he used to be. According to his own words he is most dharmic, but by his very nature he is cruel and violent. This evil man wears the cloak of dharma but is actually thoroughly caught up in false behaviour. He undertook his difficult religious austerities just to get what he wants, to get food.' When the tiger learned how the meat had been stolen, according to what they said, he commanded, 'Let the jackal be killed.'

But when the tiger's mother heard what the tiger had said, she came there to enlighten him with words for his benefit. 'My son,' she said, 'you should not accept this report, for it conceals a conspiracy to deceive you. People who are not honest are maligning someone who is honest, accusing him of faults because of their rivalry and jealousy about what he is doing. No one can bear someone who has become elevated. Rising to high position always causes hatred, and a fault is always cast upon a good person, even if he is pure. The greedy are always going to hate the pure, and cowards hate the brave. Fools hate the learned, and the poor hate the rich. Those who never follow dharma hate those who are most devoted to dharma, and the ugly hate the good-looking. Many learned people are greedy, and they all make their living through illusion and deception. They would accuse a faultless person of faults even if he had the brains of Brihaspati.

'The meat was taken from your house today when the house was empty. But the jackal didn't want it even when it was given to him. Think hard about that. Things that are false often appear to be true, and truths seem false. The sky appears to be flat, and a firefly looks like fire. But the sky is not flat, and there is no fire in a firefly. Therefore, even when you have seen something with your own eyes, it is a good idea to test it closely. And when you have tested it and you know the actual state of things, you won't regret it afterwards. My son, it is not a hard thing to do, for a ruler to have someone killed. But people prefer and praise rulers who are patient and forbearing. You established this man and made him famous among the ministers. A good man is hard to find, and you should back up this man who is your friend. For anyone who arrests a pure man who has been sullied by the accusations of other men defiles his minister and is himself soon destroyed.'

Then someone from the faction of the jackal's enemies arrived. He was a dharmic person, and he told the tiger how the deception had been made. Then the jackal's true behaviour was recognized, and he was honoured and set free. The tiger king embraced him affectionately again and again. But the jackal, who knew the science of politics, was deeply troubled by the king's betrayal of him; he took his leave of the king and wanted to fast to death. The tiger, his eyes streaming with tears because of his affection for the jackal, greatly honoured him and would not let him leave.

The jackal, seeing that the tiger was overcome with emotion out of his affection, bowed and spoke, his voice stammering with tears: 'First you honoured me, and then you dishonoured me. You delivered me into the hands of my enemies, and so I should not live with you. How can you trust me, or how can I trust you again, when you have dishonoured me and then restored my honour? You tested me, deciding that I was capable, but then you broke the agreement we had made. A person who kept his promises, if at first he talked about someone in the assembly, saying that he was virtuous, would not then denounce him as someone who lacked good qualities. How can you have confidence in me now that I have been dishonoured here? And I would be very anxious about you and have no confidence in you. You would be worried and I would be afraid, and our enemies would see the chink in our armour. What is broken is hard to put back together, and what has been put together is not hard to break. The friendship that has been broken and put back together is never graced by real affection.'

The wise jackal said these things, consoling the king with words of this sort, full of dharma and *artha* and reason, and then he went to the forest. Rejecting the conciliations and supplications of the tiger king, the wise jackal fasted to death, abandoned his body, and went to heaven.

[12.112]

17. How the Jackal Ate the Lazy Camel

Unlike the wise and virtuous jackal in the previous story, the jackal in the following tale is true to the stereotype: greedy and pitiless.

The Text

Yudhishthira asked, 'What should a king do? And what can he do to be happy?' Bhishma replied: 'Well, I will tell you what a king must do in this world, and what he can do to be happy. But you must not behave like the camel whose adventure we have heard about. Listen to it.'

Once, a great camel was born who remembered his former lives. He generated great *tapas* in the forest and undertook very severe vows. At the end of his *tapas*, Brahma became pleased with him and had him choose a boon. The camel said, 'My lord, through your favour, let my neck be so long that it can go to graze a hundred leagues in front of me.' 'So be it,' said the god, granting this superb boon, and the camel went to his own forest. But because the fool had obtained that boon, he indulged in idleness. Deluded by Time, the idiot didn't want to move to graze.

One day, stretching out his neck for a hundred leagues, he grazed with a heart that never tired of grazing. But then a great wind arose. The camel put his head and neck into a cave, while his body remained outside. Then a great rain flooded the world. And a jackal, hungry and exhausted, tormented by the rain, his body racked with cold, quickly entered that cave with his wife. When the jackal, who lived on flesh, saw the neck of the camel, he started to eat it. When the camel realized that he was being eaten, he was very unhappy, and he made an effort to draw back his neck. But however much the camel flung his neck up and down, so much more the jackal and his wife ate it. Then the jackals killed and ate the camel, and when the rain had ended, they went out by the mouth of the cave.

That is how the stupid camel met his disastrous end. See the terrible thing that eventually happens to someone who is lazy.

[12.113]

18. How the Sage turned his Dog into a Series of Larger and Larger Animals, and Finally Back into a Dog

This tale sounds a warning against ambition and self-transformation, demonstrating that blood will tell, that you can't change your caste. It is a parable against upward mobility. (In this it may be contrasted with the story of the jackal who succeeded in changing from a cowardly carnivore to a virtuous vegetarian, in 'How the Tiger's Mother Saved the Pious Jackal'.) Forest sages are said to live on fruits and roots, but the dog-sage reveals his irretrievably canine nature by living on fruits and roots—and garbage. In the end he is undone by a *sharabha*, a mythical eight-legged beast, part lion and part bird, with his eyes on the top of his head.

The Text

Bhishma said, 'They tell this old story as an example of the sort of thing that good men can do in the world. I heard the great sages tell it to make that very point.'

In a certain great forest where there were no other humans,

a sage lived on roots and fruits, restraining his senses with great control. At peace, pure, devoted only to his studies, he had purified his soul with fasting and was constantly steadfast on the right path. As that wise man sat there, all the creatures who lived in the forest came into his presence—lions and tigers and bears, *sharabhas*, great elephants in rut, leopards, rhinos, and other fierce animals. All of them, though flesh-eaters, asked about the sage's welfare, doing favours for him and prostrating themselves before him as if they were his pupils. And then they all went back as they had come.

But there was one animal there, a village dog, who never left the great sage. He was a passionate devotee, and he became weak and thin from his constant fasting and living on fruits and roots and garbage. Calm and learned, he seemed just like a pupil. When the great sage was seated, the dog lay at the base of his feet like a dog; but his temperament was like that of a human, and he was deeply bound to the sage by affection.

Then a powerful, wicked, cruel, flesh-eating leopard came there for the dog, like Time the Ender, thirsty, licking his chops, lashing his tail; his jaws were gaping; oppressed by hunger, he was after flesh. When the dog saw that cruel beast coming at him, he said to the sage, in the hope of saving his life, 'Good sir, a leopard, who is the enemy of dogs, is here and wants to kill me. Please keep me out of danger from him!' The sage said, 'Do not have any fear at all of being killed by the leopard. My little son, you will shed this form of a dog and become a leopard.' Then the dog became a leopard, with a golden form and a glittering, spotted body, and he lived joyously in the forest without fear.

But then there came a tiger, enormous and horrible, driven by hunger, licking the corners of his gaping mouth, baring his great fangs in his lust for blood as he came at the leopard. When the leopard saw that hungry, toothy tiger roaming the forest, he went to the sage for refuge, hoping to save his own life. And so, out of the affection born of constantly living together, the sage changed that leopard into a tiger more powerful than his enemies. And when the other tiger saw that, he did not attack him.

But when the dog had become a tiger, powerful and flesh-eating, he no longer had a taste for fruits and roots as his food. That dog-tiger acted just like the tiger who is king of the beasts, constantly lying in wait for the animals that live in the forest. And one day, when the dog-tiger was sleeping, lying at the door of the hut, sated by his meal of the deer he had killed, an elephant in rut came to that spot, roaring deeply like a thundering cloud. He was tall and spotted, with a large body and fine tusks, and the temple on his broad head was broken open with the flowing rut. When the tiger saw that rutting bull elephant coming at him, mad with lust, in terror of the elephant he sought refuge with the sage. The sage turned the dog-tiger into a bull elephant, like a great cloud, and when the other elephant saw him, he was afraid. The dog-elephant then wandered about happily among the lotus thickets, streaked with lotus pollen. Time passed as he took his pleasure cheerfully night after night, roaming about near the sage's hut.

But then a lion with a tawny mane came to that place, a terrifying lion born in a mountain cave, a killer of whole herds of elephants. When the dog-elephant, who was terrified of lions, saw that lion coming at him, he trembled in terror and sought refuge with the sage. And so the sage made the dog-elephant into a lion, who looked down upon the wild lion as coming from a lineage of lower birth. And when the wild lion saw the dog-lion, his roar and his strength were paralysed by fear, and he disappeared. The dog-lion went on living happily in the ashram in that forest. But the other, smaller wild animals that lived in that forest were no longer seen there, as they were terrified and in constant fear for their lives.

One day, in the fullness of Time, there came wandering through the forest a *sharabha*, eight-legged, powerful, drinking the blood of wounds, terrifying all sorts of creatures, bent on injuring all creatures that breathe. He came to the dwelling of that sage to kill the lion there. The sage made the dog-lion into a *sharabha* bursting with power, and when the wild *sharabha* saw the sage's *sharabha* in front of him, powerful and extremely fierce, he quickly ran away in terror. And the dog-*sharabha* stayed constantly at the sage's side and enjoyed the happiness of a *sharabha*.

But all the herds of wild animals were terrified of the dog-*sharabha*, and in terror they ran out of the forest in all directions, hoping to save their lives. As for the *sharabha* who had been born in the womb of a dog, he was now entirely depraved and constantly lusted to kill creatures with the breath of life in them. He became a flesh-eater and no longer wanted the peaceful food of fruits and roots. But then that ungrateful *sharabha*, driven by the powerful lust for blood, wanted to kill the sage. The sage, however, who was very wise, knew of this through the power of his *tapas* and his eye of wisdom, and he said to the dog, 'When you were a dog, you became a leopard, and as a leopard you became a tiger. The tiger became a rutting elephant, and the elephant became a lion. The lion, who had extraordinary strength, then became a *sharabha*. Because I was seduced by affection, I didn't consider your line of descent from your family. But since you are wicked and wish to harm me in this way, though I have done no wrong, you have reverted to your own breed, and so you will be nothing but a dog.'

And then, because that evil-minded, stupid creature (who had had the shape of a dog and now was a *sharabha*) hated sages, the sage cursed him, and he once again resumed his own form, a dog. And when that dog had regained his own true nature, he became absolutely miserable. The sage spoke a magic syllable and expelled the evil creature from his *tapas* forest.

[12.117–118.1]

19. How the Fish with Presence of Mind and the Farsighted Fish Survived, and the Dilatory Fish Died

Unlike the regal tiger and cunning jackal and loyal dog, to whom the folktales often attribute particular stereotypical qualities regarded as innate in their species, there is nothing particularly piscine about the fishes in this story, other than the peculiar physical circumstances of their dilemma. They seem, rather, just to represent, quite arbitrarily, three human types. The word I have translated as 'dilatory' (*dirghasutra*) more literally means 'stretching out a thread', and has a negative tone that distinguishes it from the more positive 'procrastinator' who kept Gautama from killing his wife.[20]

The Text

Bhishma said, 'Listen with full attention to this story about the consequences of being dilatory in making a decision about what should and should not be done.'

In a pond that was not very deep, there lived three fish who were friends. Among the great mass of fish, they always hung out together in the water. Now, of these three, one had the presence of mind always to know when the time to do something had arrived; another was farsighted; and the third was dilatory.

One day, fishermen used various means to drain the lower parts of the pond. The farsighted fish, realizing that the pond was vanishing to a dangerous degree, said to his two friends, 'This is a disaster that has befallen all who live in the water. Let us quickly go somewhere else before our escape path is destroyed. For the one who, with wise policies, checks an unfortunate event before it happens, never hesitates. Please, let us go.' But the dilatory fish who was there said, 'Well said, but it is my considered opinion that there is no need to hurry yet.' And the one who had presence of mind said to the farsighted one, 'When the proper time comes, I will not neglect to do what is needed.'

When the wise, farsighted fish had heard this, he left through one remaining stream and went out into the deep water.

Now, when the fishermen saw that all the water had flowed out of the pond, they caught the fish with various methods. The dilatory fish was caught along with all the other fish. The fish with presence of mind saw that the fish were being hooked and strung together on lines, and so he went among the other fish and took the line in his mouth. Pulling him up when he had taken the rope in his mouth, the fishermen thought that he too had been hooked like all the others. And when they were washing all the fish in clear water, the one with presence of mind let go of the rope and quickly swam free. But the dilatory fish, who was slow-witted and stupid, paralysed and senseless, went to his death.

And so, anyone who is so deluded that he does not realize when the right time has come is quickly destroyed, like the dilatory fish. And anyone who does not do what is best at the beginning, because he thinks, 'I am so clever,' gets into trouble, like the fish with presence of mind. But a man who takes measures to control a problem that has not yet arrived—he achieves what is best by far, like the farsighted fish.

[12.135]

20. How the Mouse Escaped from the Cat, the Owl, the Mongoose, and the Hunter

The mouse in this story is genuinely mouse-like in his relationship with other animals, and in his perilous problems, but his true persona is that of a brilliant political adviser. In the frame, Bhishma answers Yudhishthira's rather explicit question at some length, with appropriate citations from the Machiavellian *Arthashastra*, which I have omitted here in order to get straight to the story.

The Text

Yudhishthira asked, 'How can a king survive when he is weak and is surrounded by powerful enemies on all sides, when he is all alone without any allies?' Bhishma said, 'About that they tell this ancient story about a conversation between a cat and a mouse under a banyan tree.'

In a certain great forest, there was a very big banyan tree, covered over by nets of vines, where flocks of various kinds of birds roosted. Its trunks were like clouds, offering a most welcome cool shade, and deer and beasts of prey crowded around it. A very wise mouse named Palita ['Grey'] had made in its roots a hole with a thousand openings, and there he lived.

Now, from earlier times, a cat named Lomasha ['Hairy'] had lived there happily in the tree's branches, destroying the lives of the birds. A Chandala hunter always came there and laid his snares as the sun set. Setting out his nets made of sinews, he would then go home and sleep comfortably until the night gave way to dawn. All sorts of wild animals were caught there at night all the time. And one day, the cat got careless and was caught there. The cat was the mouse's enemy, always trying to kill him, and so when the cat was caught, the wise mouse, seizing the opportunity, moved about fearlessly.

As the mouse wandered about in that forest with complete confidence, looking for food, he saw, not far off, the meat that had trapped the cat. Climbing onto the trap, he then ate the meat, laughing in his mind at his enemy who was caught beneath him. But though the mouse was entirely intent upon that meat, he looked around at one moment and saw that another horrible enemy of his had arrived there. This was a mongoose named Harika ['Thief'], yellow-eyed, agile, lurking in a great hole. He had hastened there because he had smelled the mouse, and he stood on the ground, facing upwards, licking his chops at the thought of food. The mouse then saw yet another enemy, one who had alighted on a branch, an owl named Chandraka ['Moon'], a night-roamer with a sharp beak, who lived in the hollow of the tree.

As the mouse was now in great danger, in range of both the mongoose and the owl, he worried, 'In this dire emergency, with danger arising on all sides and death so near, what can one do to survive?' Threatened in this way, with the same grim outlook in every direction, he was terrified, but he devised this best possible course: 'There are multiple possibilities of disaster and destruction, and just one chance in a hundred of living. The danger of disaster confronts me on all sides. If I go to the ground, the mongoose will immediately grab me. But the owl will get me if I stay here, and the cat will get me if it breaks out of the trap. Nevertheless, a wise person like me should not give way to paralysing uncertainty. I will make every effort to live as long as I have breath in me. Those who have intelligence and are wise and learned in the science of politics do not panic even when they encounter disaster.

'How can I save my life today when three enemies are after me? I don't see any way out of this now, except the cat. I will make use of this enemy, the cat, for he is in trouble and I can do him a great service. I will ensure the cat's welfare by making use of the science of Kshatriyas, the science of politics, and so I will deceive this collection of enemies by a plan I've already made. The cat, the worst of my enemies, is in the greatest danger. If it is possible, I must get this fool to undertake an alliance for his own welfare. Now that he has encountered a disaster, he might make a treaty with me. The experts say that a person in a tight spot, if he wishes to save his life, should seek help even from an enemy, as long as that enemy is closely allied and powerful. For a learned enemy is better than an ignorant friend. My life depends on this cat who is my enemy. So be it! I will start talking with him about ways in which to protect himself. Maybe even this enemy of mine will learn something through our association.'

And so the mouse, who knew how to achieve his ends, to get what he wanted, who knew the time for making an alliance and the time for fighting, spoke to the cat, beginning with words of conciliation: 'I speak to you in friendship, Cat. Are you alive? For I want you to live, which would be the best thing for both of us together. Gentle sir, you must not despair. You will live, as before. I will save you. I would even give up my life's breaths for your sake. There is a certain way to do this, an excellent way that has occurred to me, whereby you can be set free, and I too will get what is best for me. I saw this means as I thought about myself, but what is for my benefit and also for your benefit is the best thing in common for both of us. For this mongoose-and-owl combination is evil-minded. Cat, I am safe right now, as they are not going after me. But this hooting and shifty-eyed owl is looking at me, and as I am hanging onto the branch of the tree, he terrifies me.

'It takes just seven steps together for good men to make a friendship. You are my learned housemate. I will protect our shared house so that you are not in danger of dying. For, Cat, you are not able to cut through the snare without me. I will cut through your snare—if you will not harm me. You live at the top of this banyan tree, and I shelter at its root. The two of us have certainly lived here for a long time in this tree, as you know. Someone whom no one trusts, and someone who trusts no one—wise men do not approve of either of them, for they are always uneasy in their minds. Therefore, let our friendship grow, and let there be a good agreement between us. For learned men do not wait to approve what is done only when the right time for it has passed, making it useless. Know that my plan is profitable, reasonable, and appropriate to the situation. I want you to live, and you want me to live. Someone may cross a very deep great river by means of a piece of wood; he carries the piece of wood across, and he is carried across by the piece of wood. In the same way, this union between us will benefit us both: I will save you, and you will save me.'

When the mouse had spoken in this way, full of good sense and for the benefit of both of them, with good arguments, making points worthy of persuasion, he waited for a while, impatiently. Then his clever enemy, the cat, hearing this eloquent statement, replied with good and persuasive arguments. He was intelligent and well-spoken, and he praised and quoted the other's speech and honoured him in return with conciliation, realizing that the circumstances were desperate. The cat, with his sharply pointed teeth and eyes like cats'-eye gems, looked lazily at the mouse and said, 'Good sir, bless you. I bow to you who wish to save my life. If you know what is best, do it and do not delay! For I am in serious trouble, but you are in even more trouble than I am. Let there be an agreement between the two of us without delay, for we are both in trouble. Do what must be done for the present moment, so that the two of us may succeed. And when I am freed from this tight spot, what you have done will not be forgotten. I am your devotee, your disciple, who will do whatever is best for you. I will obey your commands, for I come to you, sir, for refuge.'

When he heard this, the mouse then spoke to the cat, who was now in his power. His speech was full of good sense and very much to the point: 'What you have said so generously is not unusual for someone like you. I will follow you whenever you attack. But now I am in great danger from the mongoose. Save me and do not kill me, for I am able to set you free. And protect me from the owl, for that vile creature is always after me. I will cut loose your snares, my friend; I swear this to you in all truth.'

When the cat heard that speech that was apt and to the point, he looked at the mouse in joy and honoured him and welcomed him. And when he had thoroughly honoured the mouse and stood firm in their friendship, the cat, thinking carefully, said, firmly, affectionately, and in some haste: 'Please come quickly! You are my wise friend, equal to my very life's breaths. For through your favour, I will quickly get my life back. Whatever

I can do for you when I am in such a condition, command me and I will do it. Let there be such an agreement between the two of us as friends. When you have freed me from this danger, I—together with my relatives and my host of friends—will do everything that will please you and be for your benefit. And once I am freed from this calamity, my dear friend, and able to repay you, I will be yours, and I will do whatever you please.'

When the mouse had made the cat accept what was for its own benefit, he was quite confident and wholeheartedly began to achieve his purposes. The learned mouse, thus encouraged by the cat, confidently lay down upon the cat's chest as if the cat were his mother or father. When the mongoose and the owl saw that the mouse was nestled among the limbs of the cat, they became discouraged and went home. And the mouse, who knew about time and place, nestled among the cat's limbs and cut through the snares slowly, slowly, waiting for the right time. The cat, tormented by his bonds, seeing the mouse cutting the snares without hurrying, was in a terrible hurry. As the mouse continued to cut the snares, without hurrying, the cat then began to urge him on: 'My dear friend, why aren't you hurrying? Are you reluctant to accomplish your goal? Killer of enemies, cut the snares before the Chandala hunter, the dirty dog-cooker, comes.'

When the mouse, who had made his plans, heard these words from the cat who was in such a hurry, he said to the imprudent cat—who was under his control—these words that were in the mouse's own interest: 'Be quiet, sir; don't hurry and don't get all upset. We are the ones who understand the right time for this; we are not forgetting about the time. An enterprise undertaken at the wrong time does not accomplish its goal; undertaken at the precise time, it achieves a great goal. If you are set free at the wrong time, you will be a danger to me. Therefore, wait for the right time; why are you in such a hurry, my friend? As soon as I see the Chandala coming with his knife in his hand, then I will cut through your noose, for our common danger will have arrived. When you are set free then, you will climb the tree, for you will have no goal but to save your life. When you are frightened then and have run away, you will go out on a branch, and I will enter my hole.'

When the cat had heard the mouse tell him this, he realized that the mouse was very smart and wanted to save his own life. And as the cat was eager to do what was best for himself, he behaved correctly and modestly and said to the mouse, who was still delaying his action, 'Good people do not do generous favours for their friends like that. When I freed you from your danger I hurried. You should secure my welfare by hurrying in the very same way. You are very clever; try to assure the safety of both of us. Or are you delaying because you remember our former enmity? But see! The karma of my evil deeds has clearly led to the shortening of my lifespan. And you must not keep in your mind whatever unfriendly act I may have committed, in my ignorance, in the past. Be generous and forgive me.'

The mouse, who was wise and knew the texts, replied to the cat with this excellent speech: 'Cat, I have heard what you said as you were grasping at what was best for you. But you must realize that I too am grasping at what is best for me. A person who has made a dangerous friendship must stay carefully on guard, just as one must guard one's hand if it is near the mouth of a snake. If a person has made an agreement with someone more powerful and does not protect himself, it will do him harm, like bad food. No one is anyone's enemy. No one is anyone's friend. Motives are bound to motives. When what was to be done has been done, no one cares who did it. Therefore, one should do all the things that have to be done but leave something over to be done. At the moment when you will be terrified of the Chandala, you will be so intent on escaping that you will not be able to grab me. The majority of the ropes have been cut, but there is one rope remaining. I will cut that one, too, very fast, Lomasha. Be patient.' The two of them, both in danger, continued to talk like that.

But when the night was over, Lomasha the cat again became afraid. Then, at dawn, the Chandala appeared, grotesque, black and tawny, bald, nasty, with broad buttocks, pointed ears, an enormous mouth, a horrible face, hoary, with his sword in his hand, surrounded by a circle of dogs. He looked like a messenger from Yama the god of hell. When the cat saw him, he was terrified, and in his terror he said to the mouse, 'What will you do now?'

Now, when the mongoose and the owl also saw that horrible looking person, they too immediately became terrified and despaired. But those two intelligent and strong animals, the cat and the mouse, had closed ranks and, because of that wise policy, could not be overwhelmed by force. Seeing that the cat and the mouse had made an agreement in order to accomplish their purpose, the mongoose and the owl quickly went each to his own home.

Then the mouse cut the cat's last rope, and once the cat was freed, he ran right up the tree. The mouse was freed from his great danger, freed by his terrible enemy. He entered his hole, and the cat settled on his branch. The Chandala looked everywhere, but his hopes had been dashed in a moment. He took up his snare and went away from that place and back to his own home.

Now the cat had been freed from that danger and his own life had been saved, under very difficult conditions. Remaining on the top of the tree, he said to the mouse, who was staying in his hole, 'I ran away suddenly, without engaging in any conversation at all. But you should certainly not doubt that I am grateful, for you did me a great favour. You came to trust me and you gave me my very life. But now that it is the time to enjoy our friendship, why don't you approach me? Wise one, be my minister, and command me as if you were my father. You are in no danger from us, I swear by my own life.'

When the cat had said these words of supreme conciliation to the mouse, the mouse, who knew the cat's ultimate objectives, replied with these smooth words about what was for his own benefit: 'Lomasha, I've heard all that you've said; now listen as I tell you how it seems to me. Friends can take the form of enemies, and enemies can take the form of friends. No one is born an enemy, nor is a friend simply found. They become friends and enemies because of the interaction of their abilities and their goals. There is no permanent friendship, nor any enduring enmity. A friend may become an enemy in the course of the vicissitudes of time, and an enemy may become a friend. Self-interest is the most powerful factor. A mother and a father will abandon their own beloved son if he has fallen; people protect themselves—this is the essence of self-interest.

'You speak honeyed words—"You are dear to me"—but all of that is lying. What reason is there for me to think that I am dear to you? We know of none, other than for the sake of becoming your food. For a while, in the past, as long as there was a cause, we two were friends. But that friendship disappeared along with the cause that was determined by the moment in time. For you are my perpetual and ultimate enemy, and only our shared goal made us friends. When that task was ended, our natures reverted to their enmity. You have no other purpose at all for me other than eating me. I am the food and you are the eater; I am weak and you are strong. Given this uneven power, there can be no alliance between us. I admire your intelligence, so that immediately after being set free you are hunting for something to eat, which is doubtless what you need to be happy. But you were caught because you were after food, and as soon as you got free you went out, hungry. And you are trying to make an alliance with me today in order to eat me, though I am a person who knows the textbooks. For I know that you are hungry and that it is your feeding time. Once you've made an alliance with me, you will hunt me again to eat me. If your dear wife and your sons see you united with me, how would they not eat me quite happily, thrilled and affectionate though they may be to see you?'

As the mouse went on talking in this way, the cat became nervous. Quickly he went into his own hole. Then the wise mouse went to another hole. And thus the mouse overcame many powerful enemies because, though he was weak and alone, he was wise and smart.

[12.136]

21. How Vishvamitra Tried to Eat a Dalit's Dog

In the following story, a dog is not a subject but an object, indeed a highly symbolic object.

We have encountered a number of low caste people in these stories, primarily the outcaste (now called Dalit) hunters known as Chandalas, who are often called 'dog-cookers' (Shva-paka), a word that is usually employed as a term of abuse but that is literally true in the story we are about to consider. This story takes place in the last of the four Ages, the present age, the Kali Yuga, a time in which human evil flourishes. This is also a time of *apad* dharma, the dharma that one should follow in time of great disaster and emergency (*apad*). (The whole subsection of Book Twelve in which this story and two others in this collection[21] appear is called the *apad*-dharma section.) We have heard the story of Vishvamitra's peculiar birth in the tale of 'How Satyavati's Mother Corrupted Her Daughter's Pregnancy'. Here he fulfils his father's worst fears for him.

The Text

Yudhishthira asked Bhishma how a Brahmin can survive in the Kali Yuga, the last of the four Ages, when dharma has become adharma, when there are no rains, and bandits have stolen all the food. And he asked how a king should conduct himself, without losing artha or dharma, when the world has become polluted. Bhishma replied, 'When a time arrives that brings harm and crime to a king's subjects, they must use their powers of discrimination in order to live. And on this subject they tell this ancient history of a conversation between Vishvamitra and a Chandala in the Chandala's hut.'

Once upon a time, it happened through the workings of fate that there was a horrible drought that lasted for twelve years. Indra sent no rain, and the planet Jupiter moved in a retrograde direction. The moon's markings became invisible as it moved along a southern path. There was not even any dew at the end of the night, let alone any streaks of clouds. The flow of water in the rivers slowed to a trickle and in some places dried up altogether. Bones and skulls were strewn about, and crowds of ghosts moaned aloud. The cities were almost entirely empty, and the houses in the villages were burnt. Most places were empty of all their people, sometimes because of thieves, sometimes because of corrupt kings, and because people were afraid of one another. At this terrifying time, when dharma was vanishing, mortals starved and ate one another. The sages abandoned their vows, their ritual fires, and their gods. Leaving their ashrams, they wandered about here and there.

Now, the great and wise sage Vishvamitra, who never had a house, was assailed by hunger and wandered all about. One day in the forest he happened to come to a village of dog-cookers, cruel killers of living creatures. The place was strewn about with broken pots and dog-skins, with heaps of the shattered bones of boars and donkeys, and great piles of jugs made of human skulls. It was littered with the garments of the dead, with garlands and ornaments left over from funerals, and the huts were hung with the sloughed skins of snakes. The altars of the gods had iron bells and flags made of owls' feathers; packs of dogs surrounded them.

The great sage Vishvamitra entered that place; oppressed by hunger, he made a great effort in his determination to search for food. But as he begged, he found nothing there, not meat or rice or roots or fruits or anything else at all. He thought, 'Alas! I have fallen upon a terrible misfortune.' And because of his weakness he fell to the ground in that village of Chandalas. And he thought, 'I must have some good karma left. How can I avoid such a meaningless death?'

Then the sage saw, spread out in one Chandala's house, some dog-flesh, newly butchered with a knife and hung on a rope. And he thought, 'I must steal this from here. For there is now no other way for me to save my life. The rule is that in times of emergency [*apad*], a person who is superior may steal from one who is inferior, and it proceeds step by step: At first, one should take from someone inferior, and then from an equal. But if these do not exist, one can take even from a superior person who obeys dharma. If, therefore, I take from the household of those who live on the margins, I do not see any sin of theft. I will take this meat.'

When he had made this wise decision, Vishvamitra went to sleep right in the place where he had fallen. When he saw that it was deep night, and that the entire Chandala village was asleep, he got up quietly and went into the hut. The Chandala seemed fast asleep, his eyes pasted shut with mucus; he looked horrible and filthy. But then he spoke with a broken, harsh voice and said, 'Who is pulling on my dirty rope when the Chandala village is asleep? I am not asleep; I'm awake and cruel, and you are a dead man.' 'I am Vishvamitra!' the sage said to him, abruptly, for he had been suddenly overcome by terror and was horrified by what he had done.

When the Chandala heard the words of the great sage, he scrambled up from his bed in great confusion. With tears flowing from his eyes, he cupped his hands in reverence and said to Vishvamitra, 'Brahmin, what are you trying to do in the night?' Vishvamitra said to the Chandala, reassuring him, 'I am starving today, at the end of my life's breath, and I am going to steal this haunch of a dog. As my life's breaths are subsiding, hunger is destroying my memory. Even though I am well aware of my own dharma, I am going to steal this haunch of a dog. For however much I wandered around, I couldn't find anything to eat until I came to your house. I set my mind on committing an evil act. A thirsty man will drink foul water; there is no shame in someone desperately seeking food. Hunger corrupts dharma. I am going to steal this haunch of a dog. Fire, whose feet are clean, is the mouth of the gods and their sacrificial priest. Know that I am, like him, omnivorous, because of my dharma, though I am a Brahmin.'

The Chandala said to him, 'Sage, listen to what I say, and when you've heard me, act in such a way that you will not violate dharma. Wise men proclaim that a dog is the lowest of animals, and the very worst part of a dog's body is the thigh and hindquarters. Great sage, you didn't think about this perverse action very well, stealing from a Chandala and especially stealing something that should not be eaten. Think of some other, good means of saving your life; don't destroy all your *tapas* because of your lust for meat. This is a forbidden path; don't abandon dharma, for you are one of the supreme authorities on dharma.'

Vishvamitra, tormented by hunger, replied, 'I have spent a long time running about, without anything to eat. I haven't found any way to stay alive. A person in desperation should manage to stay alive by whatever action he can, no matter what. He should act within dharma if he can. The dharma of Kshatriyas comes from Indra, and that of Brahmins comes from Fire. The fire of Brahma is my strength, and I will eat whenever I am hungry. For whatever one can do to stay alive should be done, and not unwillingly. Living is better than dying; one can only achieve dharma when one is alive. And since I desire to live, I will even eat what should not be eaten. I thought about this earlier and made my decision; grant me this. Living, I will act within dharma and will drive away all things inauspicious with my *tapas* and my knowledge, just as the celestial bodies dispel the great darkness.' And Vishvamitra, having made up his mind, stole the dog's hindquarter. To save his life, the great sage grabbed the haunch and went to the forest with his wife.

Now, at this very time, Indra sent rain, reviving all the

creatures and making the grasses grow. And after a long time, Vishvamitra burnt away all his sins with his *tapas*, and achieved supreme success.

And so, if a learned man encounters a disaster and wants to live, and his heart does not despair, and if he knows a lot of expedients, he saves himself, however wretched he may be. A man should always use his head to stay alive, and when he lives, he gains merit and achieves happiness and prosperity. A wise man uses his intelligence to distinguish between dharma and the violation of dharma, and he lives on in this world.

[12.139]

22. How the Heron King Saved the Ungrateful Brahmin

The Brahmin villain in this story lives among people sometimes called *dasyus* (foreigners, slaves or barbarians), sometimes *shabaras* (tribals, savages or barbarians) or *mlecchas* (foreigners, non-Sanskrit-speakers or barbarians). I will translate all these terms as 'barbarian'. Some caste lines are crossed in this story in interesting ways. The actual barbarian is kind, generous, and pious; he keeps his promises and is good to Brahmins. The Brahmin, by contrast, is the low one, dark-skinned—usually a sign of base, non-Brahminic birth, in texts of this period, ignorant of the Veda, and cruel. His marriage to a widow who is a Shudra is regarded as a doubly serious sin. (Though he is named Gautama, he is no relation to the Gautama whose wife Indra seduced, let alone Gautama Shakyamuni the Buddha; Gautama is a fairly common name.) His one saving grace is his pure line of descent, which he traces back to Kashyapa, a great and famous ancient sage. In this story, however, Kashyapa is also the ancestor of the Rakshasas, making the vicious Brahmin Gautama a relative of the Rakshasa king—but, in yet another moral surprise, the Rakshasa king is virtuous and gentle.

Much else, too, is topsy-turvy here. Herons are usually regarded as religious hypocrites (who seem to be meditating vegetarians but then suddenly strike out and gobble up little fishes), and Rakshasas as blood-sucking demons. But not here! Here, the heron sacrifices himself for his ungrateful friend. And here the Rakshasas have a higher moral code than the barbarians; the Rakshasas won't eat the dead sinner but give him to the barbarians to eat. The villainous Brahmin continues to get away with evil again and again until the very end, when he finally gets his comeuppance in hell.

The Text

Yudhishthira asked Bhishma about people who are ungrateful to their friends. In his response, Bhishma alluded to a particular story, and Yudhishthira said, 'I want to hear in detail about the ungrateful man who injured his friend.' Bhishma said: 'I will tell you this ancient story that took place in the Northern country, where the barbarians live.'

There was a Brahmin named Gautama who lived in the middle country. He was dark-skinned and had not studied the Veda. One day he came to a village that was full of people; he entered it, hoping to beg for alms. There lived there a rich barbarian who knew the distinctions between all the classes; he kept his promises, took pleasure in giving, and was pious and good to Brahmins. The Brahmin went to the barbarian's house and begged for alms; he asked for a place of shelter where he could live, and enough alms to live for a year. The barbarian gave the Brahmin all of this as well as a garment that seemed to be new and a Shudra woman of some years who had been abandoned by her husband and widowed, and who now married Gautama. The Brahmin Gautama cheerfully accepted all this from the barbarian; he took his pleasure with the woman in that excellent house. He even helped the barbarian out with his household chores and lived happily in the barbarian's prosperous house throughout the rains.

Gautama then made a great effort to learn the art of archery. He constantly killed all the geese that came within range of his arrows, just as the band of barbarians did. Intent upon violence, devoid of pity, Gautama always took pleasure in killing living creatures. From his close association with the barbarians, he became like them. Many months passed as he lived happily like that in the village of the barbarians, killing many birds.

Then one day another Brahmin came to that country, to the village of barbarians where Gautama lived; he came from the same country as Gautama and had been his close friend. But this Brahmin had matted locks and wore a garment of rags and antelope hides; he was pure, humble, intent upon his studies; he restricted what he ate; he had mastered the Vedas and kept his vow of chastity. He sought the house of a Brahmin, as he would have nothing to do with Shudras. Then that fine Brahmin entered Gautama's house, and when Gautama later arrived there, the two of them met. Gautama's hands were loaded down with geese, and he was holding his bow; his body was smeared with blood as he came through the door of the house.

When the Brahmin saw him, and saw that he looked like a cannibal, degraded and reviled, he still recognized him and was embarrassed. But he said, 'Why are you behaving in this insane way? For you are a Brahmin from a good family, well known in the middle country. How did you become a barbarian? Remember the Brahmins who went before you, in whose lineage you were born; they were famous masters of the Veda, and now you are a disgrace to the lineage. Awaken yourself and remember your truth and virtue and learning and generosity and compassion. Leave this dwelling place, Brahmin.'

Gautama knew that his friend had said this out of his wish to do what was best for him; he thought hard, and replied, in great misery, 'I have no wealth, and no knowledge of the Vedas. Understand that I came here in search of a way to make my living. But seeing you has made me realize that I can do no more here. Let us spend the night here and tomorrow morning return together to our true selves as proper Brahmins.'

But when that night was over, and the good Brahmin had gone, Gautama went out and headed for the ocean. He saw some ocean-going merchants standing by the path, and he joined their caravan. In a mountain cavern, the caravan was attacked by an elephant in rut and was almost entirely destroyed. The Brahmin somehow escaped from that caravan; not knowing what direction to take, he ran away to the north, to save his life. He lost everything—the caravan, his money, his country. All alone, he ran about there in the forest like a wild man. Then he found a path that led in the direction of the ocean, and he reached a charming forest, full of large flowering trees, with groves of mango trees flowering in all seasons, like the forest of heaven. There were all sorts of sweet-scented trees—palm trees, cinnamon trees, aloes and sandalwood. Everywhere there was melodic birdsong. And there were birds with human faces, living near the ocean. The Brahmin Gautama listened to the sweet sound of the birds, and then he left.

He saw a level place covered with sweet-smelling golden sand, like a piece of heaven. And he saw a great banyan tree with so many branches that it was like an umbrella. Its roots were spread with chips of superb sandalwood, and it was covered with divine flowers, like the throne of Brahma. When Gautama saw that tree, he was delighted; he went to it joyously and sat down underneath it. As he was sitting there, a pleasant, pure wind blew, rippling the flowers and refreshing all his limbs. The Brahmin was exhausted, but when that auspicious breeze touched him, he felt happy, and he slept.

When the sun had set, and twilight came on, the king of birds, king of the herons, came there to his own home from the world of his dear friend Brahma. He was known as Rajadharma; he was the wise son of a divine maiden, and he was as gorgeous as the king of the gods. He was covered in gold, adorned on all his limbs with ornaments that shone like the sun. When Gautama saw him, he was astonished, but as he was overcome by thirst and hunger, he wanted to harm him.

Rajadharma said, 'Welcome to you, Brahmin! It is fortunate that you have come to my house. The sun has set and now twilight is coming on. You will be honoured as a beloved and blameless guest with all the guest rituals tonight, and then you can leave in the morning. I am descended from the sage Kashyapa. Welcome to you, good Brahmin!' When Gautama heard those sweet words, and looked at Rajadharma, he was amazed and full of curiosity. Rajadharma gave him the honours due to a guest, with a glorious seat decorated with flowers, and performed the ritual according to the rules. He offered him some of the many fish that swim in the rivers around the Ganges; he cooked the fat fish over a well-kindled fire. The Brahmin ate the fish and was delighted, and while he was eating, his host fanned him with his wings to stave off his exhaustion.

When Gautama was seated and rested, Rajadharma asked him about his lineage. Gautama replied, 'I am Gautama, a Brahmin,' and said nothing more. Rajadharma prepared for him a beautiful bed made of leaves and covered with sweet-smelling flowers, and Gautama laid down on it happily. As soon as Gautama was on the bed, the king of the herons asked him, 'What was your reason for coming here?' Then Gautama said to him, 'I am poor. I wanted to go to the ocean to amass some wealth.' Rajadharma, pleased, said to him, 'Don't worry. You will get what you want and will go home a wealthy man. According to Brihaspati, there are four ways to get rich: inheritance, luck, hard work and friends. I have appeared to you as a friend, and you have my friendship. And so I will see to it that you will be rich.'

At dawn, Rajadharma asked Gautama if he was comfortable and then said, 'Go, my friend, along this road and you will get what you want. When you have gone three leagues from here, you will meet the great overlord of the Rakshasas, named Virupaksha, who has a powerful army and is my friend. Go to him, in my name, and he will give you all that you desire.' So Gautama went away, no longer tired, and he ate ambrosial fruits, as much as he desired. He went quickly on that path, enjoying the trees that had bark and leaves of sandalwood, aloe and cinnamon.

Then he came to a city with gates of stone and parapets of stone and a gateway of stone. The wise king of the Rakshasas, informed that a beloved friend had sent an honoured guest, said to his servants, 'Bring Gautama immediately through the city gates.' And so men in white garments shouted through the city gate, 'Gautama!' The servants of the king of the Rakshasas said to Gautama, 'Hurry! Go quickly! The king wants to see you! The heroic king of the Rakshasas, the famous Virupaksha, is in a hurry to see you, so come quickly!' Gautama was so amazed that his exhaustion vanished, and he ran, and when he saw the wealth of the city, he was even more amazed. Together with the servants, Gautama ran quickly to the king's palace, longing for an audience [*darshan*] with the king of the Rakshasas.

Then he was announced to the king of the Rashasas, and he entered the fine palace and was honoured by the king and he sat down on an excellent chair. When he was asked about his lineage and his Vedic studies and his vow of chastity, Gautama said nothing about all that but merely told his family lineage. When the king saw that he lacked the splendour of a Brahmin, and had never studied, and knew only his family lineage, he asked him, 'Good sir, where is your dwelling place? And what is the family lineage of your Brahmin wife? Do tell me this, and don't be afraid; relax and be comfortable.' Gautama said, 'I was born in the middle country, and my dwelling place is in a barbarian's house. My wife is a Shudra, a widow who remarried. I am telling you the truth.' Then the king mused, 'How can this be? What should I do?' And as he wondered about this he worried: 'This man is a Brahmin by birth, and a friend of my noble friend, Rajadharma, who sent him to me. I will do a favour for him, for he has sought refuge with me. And he is my brother and my relative[22] and my dear friend. Today is the full moon in the month of Kartika [October-November], and I will feed a thousand Brahmins. So I will feed this man, too, and give him some of my wealth.'

Then a thousand learned Brahmins arrived, adorned and bathed and robed in new silk. Virupaksha received them with the proper honour and the proper ritual. By his command, blankets were spread out for them on the ground, and servants distributed cushions on them. When these supreme Brahmins were seated there, the king honoured them, and they shone like so many moons. Golden platters with diamonds embedded in them, filled with the best food, flowing with honey and ghee, were given to the Brahmins.

Gautama quickly took up a heavy load of gold and left. He carried it with difficulty until he came to the banyan tree. There he sat down, exhausted and depressed and hungry. Then Rajadharma, the supreme bird, came to him and welcomed him joyously, with the affection due to a friend. The heron dispelled Gautama's exhaustion by fanning him with the tips of his wings and gave him food. No longer exhausted, Gautama ate and thought: 'Because of my greed and my confusion, I've taken up this extremely heavy burden of gorgeous gold, and I have a long way to go. And there is nothing for me to eat along this road to sustain my life's breaths. What can I do to stay alive?' He saw nothing to eat on the path. And then that ungrateful man thought to himself, 'This king of the herons is a big platter of meat standing right at my side. I will kill him and take him and go away fast.'

The king of herons had made a great blazing fire not far from Gautama, and he slept confidently beside it. But the evil-minded ingrate, Gautama, stayed awake, to kill Rajadharma. He killed the trusting heron with a blazing firebrand and rejoiced when he had killed him, for he did not see the consequences. He stripped off the wings and feathers and cooked the rest of the bird in the fire; then he took the pot of meat and the gold and quickly went away.

When another day had passed after that, the Rakshasa Virupaksha said to his son, 'My son, I haven't seen Rajadharma, that best of birds, today. Every day, the heron goes at the break of sunrise to worship Brahma, and he never leaves the house without greeting me. But for two nights and sunrises he has not come to my house, and so I am uneasy at heart. I must find out about my friend. That wretched Brahmin Gautama had given up his studies and had none of the radiance of a Brahmin; I worry that he has gone to Rajadharma and killed him. He behaved very badly, and I could tell that he was evil-minded, from his movements and other signs. He performed no rituals and looked dark and horrible, like the worst barbarian. My son, go quickly from here to the house of Rajadharma. Gautama has gone there, and that is why my mind is disturbed. Find out, without delay, if my pure-souled friend is alive.'

The wise son of the king of the Rakshasas went quickly, with some Rakshasas, to the banyan tree, where he saw Rajadharma's skeleton. The prince wept and went as fast as he could go to catch Gautama. He caught him not far from there, and he also found the body of Rajadharma, missing its wings and bones and feet. The Rakshasas seized Gautama and went quickly back to the king. They showed the king the body of Rajadharma and presented the ungrateful, evil-minded Gautama. When the king saw Rajadharma he wept, and so did his ministers and priests, and a great sound of wailing arose in his palace. The women and children in the inner citadel were disturbed in their thoughts and emotions. Then the king said to his son, 'Have this evil man killed. And let all of these people feast on his flesh, to their heart's desire. For he is evil in his conduct, evil in his actions, evil in his soul, evil in his convictions. You Rakshasas must kill him; this is my ruling.'

The fierce Rakshasas killed him but did not want to eat him. The night-wandering Rakshasas bowed their heads to the ground and said to the king of the Rakshasas, 'He is an evildoer, the lowest of men. You should not give a sinner to us to eat;

give him to the barbarians.' 'So be it,' said the king; 'let this ingrate be given to the barbarians this very day.' Then the king's servants, with tridents and clubs in their hands, cut that evil man into pieces and gave the pieces to the barbarians. But even the barbarians did not want to eat him, he had done such evil; and even the flesh-eating animals did not eat the ingrate. There is some expiation for a Brahmin-killer, for a drunkard, for a thief, or for someone who breaks his vows; but there is no expiation for an ingrate. A cruel, ungrateful man who injures his friend is the lowest of men. Even beasts of prey and worms do not eat such people.

Then the king of the Rakshasas, Virupaksha, adorned Rajadharma, the king of herons, with jewels and perfumes and many cloths, and had a funeral pyre made for him. And Virupaksha set fire to Rajadharma and performed the various funeral rituals according to the tradition.

Now, at that moment, the goddess Surabhi, the divine cow who lives in heaven, appeared above, streaming milk. A milky froth streamed from her and fell right on the funeral pyre of Rajadharma. That milk brought Rajadharma back to life; he arose and embraced Virupaksha. Then Indra, king of the gods, came to Virupaksha's city and said to Virupaksha, 'Thank goodness he is alive!' And Indra told Virupaksha an old story about a curse that Brahma had given to Rajadharma in the past: When Rajadharma had failed to approach Brahma in his palace humbly, Brahma in fury had said to him, 'Since this fool, this wretch, the worst of herons, has not come humbly to my palace, therefore he will soon be killed.' And because of Brahma's words, Gautama had killed the heron. But now, when the divine cow sprinkled the heron with the elixir of immortality, Brahma brought him back to life again.

Then Rajadharma prostrated himself before Indra and said, 'If you are inclined to do me a favour, Indra, let this most beloved friend of mine, Gautama, be brought to life too.' Indra agreed to this request; he revived Gautama and handed him over to his friend. Rajadharma approached his friend Gautama, who was still carrying the cooking pot and the bundle of gold, and embraced him with great love. Then Rajadharma took his leave of that evildoer and went back to his own home. He went to Brahma's palace, and Brahma honoured that noble bird with all the rituals of hospitality.

But Gautama went back to the barbarian's home and had, with the Shudra woman, sons who committed evil deeds. And so the gods gave him a severe curse: 'When this great ingrate has begotten sons in the womb of this wife, after a long time he will go to a great and terrible hell.' And so he did.

[12.162–7]

IV. Stories about How Evil Came Into the World

We have already considered one story, the very first story in this collection, explaining How Brahma Made Women Evil to Delude Men, and the classical Sanskrit texts tell many such stories about the origins of various aspects of evil.[23] But each text tells it differently. Here are a few more from the *Mahabharata*, which deal with the ancient problem from several different angles.

Different texts assign the task of creation in general, and of evil in particular, to different gods. Of the stories translated here, the first text regards Brahma as responsible for the original creation (as he usually is) and also for death (which Brahma is not always blamed for). And this text assumes that the world will always be burdened with the problem of death.

The second, much shorter text begins at a moment when the universe has already been created (perhaps by Brahma, as usual) but it assumes that the world was free of evil until the demons corrupted it. This, however, turns out to be not a permanent, insoluble problem (as it is in most texts, including our first text here) but a temporary lapse that is immediately corrected by the god Shiva. We must assume, however, that the correction, too, is only temporary, for we know that the Golden Age that Shiva restored invariably must yield to the corruption of time, to culminate in the present evil Kali Age that we now experience.

The third text assumes that the Kali Age is inevitable, and that the fact that people became basically evil when the Kali Age began—and that they remain so now—cannot be changed but can at least be to some extent controlled by *force majeure*. This concession is then used to justify what the text itself admits is unjust—the power of kings over other people who are, in all significant ways, just as good as the kings.

23. How Brahma Created Death, Diseases, Desire and Anger

The occasion for this story is, as so often in this text, a father's mourning for his dead son. We have seen how, to console King Srinjaya after the death of his son, Narada told him a series of stories about great kings whose sons had died. Here Narada tells such stories to console another king, Avikampaka, for a similar loss. This time, however, death is not (as in the story of Brahma's creation of women) merely created *because of* women; Death herself (a feminine noun in Sanskrit) *is* female. But she is highly virtuous, and eventually she manages to shift the blame for dying from herself onto the diseases that kill people, and even onto the people who die.

The Text

Yudhishthira said, 'These kings and warriors lie here, bereft of their life's breath, and the word "dead" is applied to them. These dead kings were generally fierce in their attack. I have begun to worry about this: What makes consciousness die? Who is the father of death? Where does death come from? Who or what makes death carry off creatures here? Tell me that.'

Bhishma said: 'Long ago, in the Golden Age, there was a king who lost his horse in battle and fell into the power of the enemy. His mighty son, as well as the army and his foot followers, all were killed by enemies in the battle. The king was overwhelmed by grief for his son. Seeking peace, he chanced to see Narada, who was wandering on earth. The king told Narada everything that had happened, how he was captured by the enemies in battle and his son had died. Then Narada told him this story, which takes away one's grieving for a son.

Your majesty, listen today to this very detailed narrative, just as it happened and just as I heard it.

When Brahma had created all the creatures, they became extremely old and numerous but did not die. There was no space between creatures at all, anywhere. The three worlds had no room to breathe, as if they had been tightly bound up. Then Brahma began to think about destroying it all, but he could not think of any reason to do this. From his anger, a fire came out of the nine openings of his body, and with that fire Brahma burnt everything in all directions. The fire born of his anger burnt heaven and earth and the sky, and the universe with everything moving and still. All were burnt by the great blast of anger when Brahma became angry.

Then Shiva went to seek refuge with Brahma, hoping to help all living creatures. Brahma said to him, 'What wish should I grant for you today? For I think you deserve a favour. I will do whatever will please you and will increase your thriving and growth.' Shiva said, 'The creatures that you created are now everywhere being burnt by the fire of your great energy. Seeing them fills me with compassion. You should not get angry with them.'

Brahma said, 'I am not angry, nor is it my wish that these creatures should not exist. But I want to reabsorb all of this in order to lighten the earth. For this goddess Earth, tormented by her burden, and sinking into the waters because of it, has kept urging me to reabsorb them all. I have thought about this with my full intelligence, but I don't understand how to reduce the number of those who have grown so numerous, and I've been overcome by anger.' Shiva said, 'Be merciful about reabsorbing everything; do not get angry. Do not destroy all the creatures. All the ponds, and all the grasses, the things that move and the things that are still—all of that has been reduced to ashes, and the whole universe has been flooded. Have mercy, lord; this is the boon I beg. These creatures who have been destroyed will never come back again. Think, therefore, of some other method, out of your desire to do what is best for your creatures, so that all these living beings may return again. Be merciful! I beg you to let these creatures come back again.'

When Brahma heard Shiva's words, he restrained his speech and thought, and he withdrew his own fiery energy that had come from within him and drew back the fire that had been born of his anger. Then, out of all the openings of his body a woman appeared. She was black, with red eyes, and the palms of her hands were red. She was wearing red garments and divine earrings and jewellery. As she came out of the openings of his body, she settled on his right side, and the two gods just looked at her. Then Brahma called to her and said, 'Death! Kill these creatures! I thought of you when I was worrying about universal destruction, and I was angry. Destroy all these creatures, the fools and the wise, without exception; for I have appointed you for this, and you will be well rewarded.'

When the goddess Death heard this, she was miserable, and as she was just a young girl, she burst into tears. Brahma caught those tears in his two hands and asked her yet again to do what was best for humans. But the weak, wide-eyed girl controlled her grief, cupped her hands, bent like a vine, and said, 'How can a woman like me, created by you, engage in such terrible work, terrifying all creatures that breathe? I'm afraid to act against dharma. Assign some work for me that is in keeping with dharma. Look upon me with a kindly eye, for I am so frightened. I should not carry off young people and old people full of the breath of life, people who have committed no offence. I bow to you. Have mercy on me! If I were to kill beloved sons, and friends, brothers, mothers and fathers, I would be afraid of them when they were dead! The floods of tears of pity would burn me for eternity. I come to you for refuge. Let those who do evil deeds go, in the end, to the house of the god of death. I beg you, grant me this boon, do me this favour: I wish to engage in *tapas*.'

Brahma said: 'Death, I imagined you for the purpose of destroying all creatures. Go. Destroy all these creatures. Do not delay. This must happen in just this way. It will not be otherwise. Do what I told you to do.' When Death heard this, she said nothing but just stood there, bending humbly and looking up at Brahma. Again and again he spoke to her, but she seemed to have lost her mental energy, and he remained silent.

Then Brahma became pacified, within himself and by himself, and he smiled and looked down upon all the worlds. And when Brahma's anger had subsided, the maiden went away from him, without having promised to destroy the creatures. We have heard that she began to engage in the most difficult *tapas*. She stood on one foot for fifteen billion years. Brahma again came to her and said, 'Death, do what I told you to do.' But, disregarding him, she immediately stood on the other foot for another seven billion years in the very same way. Then, for another fourteen billion years, she roamed with the deer, and then she went back and kept a vow of utter silence, standing in water, for eight thousand years. After that, she went to the river Kaushiki and kept her vow to eat nothing but wind and water; she went to the Ganges and Mount Meru and stood motionless like a tree; and on the peak of Himalaya, where the gods assembled, she stood on her big toe for another billion years.

Finally, she satisfied Brahma by her great effort, and he said to her, 'Why is this going on, my daughter? Do what I told you to do.' But Death replied to Brahma again, 'I will not destroy the creatures. Again I ask you to forgive me.' She was terrified of violating dharma, but Brahma said, 'There is no violation of dharma in you, Death, if you curb and control these creatures. But I will grant you what you wished for: creatures tortured by disease will not blame you. Among men you will have the form of a man; among women, the form of a woman; and among those of the third gender, you will be a "non-man".'[24] When she heard this, she cupped her hands and said 'No!' again to Brahma, but he insisted: 'Death, destroy humans. Your teardrops that I see have fallen and that you are holding in front of you in your two hands—they will become diseases that will torment humans when the proper time has come. At the time of the end, you will harness with desire and anger all creatures that have the breath of life, and in this way you will not violate dharma, for your behaviour will be equable and fair.'

Death agreed to this assignment, because she was afraid of a curse. And so, at the time of the end, desire and anger overwhelm and delude creatures that breathe, and so they destroy them. The tears that Death shed became diseases that shatter the bodies of humans, of all creatures, at the end of their life's breaths. All the gods depart and then return again just exactly as before. In this same way, all humans, at the end of their time of breathing, go away and return, just like the gods.

This is how the god Brahma created the death of living creatures, so that Death could take them away at the appointed time. The diseases are the tears that she shed; and when the right time comes, they carry away living creatures.

Therefore, your majesty, do not sorrow, but use your intelligence to understand. Do not grieve for your son; he has reached heaven and is happy.

[12.283]

24. How the Demons Destroyed Dharma, and Shiva Restored It

The story that Bhishma tells Yudhishthira in this next text does not really answer Yudhishthira's question except in a most roundabout way, contrasting the good, dharmic behaviour of the original creatures (for which they were rewarded) with the evil, *adharmic*, behaviour of the corrupted creatures (for which they were destroyed). The state of moral purity that prevails at the opening of this story matches the standard description of the Krita Yuga, the first of the four ages, but this is not a Golden Age. It is here, as always, destroyed, but this time it is restored—which is why it cannot be called the Golden Age. For that is by definition something that, as Robert Frost reminded us, can never remain.[25]

The Text

Yudhishthira asked Bhishma, 'What good action/karma should a man strive for so that he achieves what is best when he is here and when he dies? Tell me that.' Bhishma said:

It has been heard in an ancient text that the creatures were once controlled merely by the punishment of shaming. Men here on earth always praised dharma; they thrived on dharma and honoured the virtues.

But the demons, who could not bear dharma, gradually entered the creatures there. Then arrogance was born in those creatures, and that arrogance destroyed their dharma. And anger arose again and again in those who were full of arrogance. Then those overpowered by anger were full of loathing, and then, in its turn, confusion reigned. Finally, overpowered by confusion, the creatures did not see as they had before, and they crushed one another at will and became arrogant towards the gods and failed to honour the Brahmins. Now the punishment of shaming had no effect.

Then the gods sought refuge with Shiva. The demons had gone up into the sky and settled in three cities. Shiva brought their three cities down to earth with a single arrow, and with his trident he killed their fierce overlord, who had terrified the gods. When the demon overlord was killed, humans regained their own nature. And then the Vedas and the sacred texts thrived as they had in the earlier time.

[12.283]

25. How the Golden Age Disappeared, and the Sages Created the First King

Another version of the tale of the origin of evil combines the loss of Eden with another major theme: the origin of kingship. The previous text is linked to the present one by the assumption that, in the Golden Age, people simply grew tired of being good, that no villains were needed to destroy the original happy world, since evil will inevitably arise when virtue is not enforced. And who to do this enforcing but the king?

The text we are about to consider begins with what almost sounds like an anti-royalist, quasi-anarchist diatribe against kingship, spoken by King Yudhishthira himself: 'The king has hands, head and neck like those of other men, and the same intelligence and senses and soul...'[26] But it soon becomes apparent that this prelude was designed precisely in order to silence such a diatribe and to proclaim the special goodness of kings. Thus, this text about the loss of the Golden Age forms a bridge to our next section, which is all about kings—the theme at the heart of the *Mahabharata*.

The Text

King Yudhishthira cupped his hands and bowed to Bhishma and said, 'The word "King, king" is heard everywhere. How did this word arise? Tell me this. The king has hands, head and neck like those of other men, and the same intelligence and senses and soul, misery and happiness, back and arms and stomach, the same semen, bones and marrow, flesh and blood. He breathes in and out as they do, and his body and vital breaths are like theirs. And he is born and dies as they do and has the same qualities as all men. How then does one man stand over those heroes who are outstanding in their intelligence? How is it that he alone protects the whole earth even though it is overflowing with brave warriors and nobles? And that the people seek the favour of this one man? The whole world is pleased when this one man is pleased and is troubled when he is troubled. The whole universe bows down to this one person as if he were a god. I want to hear the true reason for all of this.'

Bhishma said, 'Listen with full attention to the whole story of how kingship arose, with nothing left out.'

In the beginning, in the Golden Age, there was no kingship at all, no king, no rod of punishment or anyone to wield that rod.

For all the people protected one another because of dharma. But as men guarded one another in that way, they became completely exhausted, and then confusion entered them. And when men had fallen into the power of confusion, and when the confusion had affected their intelligence, their dharma was destroyed, and they were all overpowered by greed.

Then men touched what did not belong to them, and desire arose in them, blotting out all else. Passion entered them when they had fallen into the grip of desire, and when they were overcome by emotion, they could not distinguish what should be done from what should not be done. They did not distinguish women they could approach for sex from those they could not approach, nor what could be said from what could not be said, what could be eaten or not eaten, what was a mistake or not a mistake. When this world of men had been lost in this way, the Veda was lost. And because the Veda was lost, dharma was lost.

Now, when the Veda and dharma had been lost, the gods were terrified, and in their terror they sought refuge with Brahma. Tormented by misery and sorrow and fear, all the gods reached Brahma and cupped their hands and said, 'My lord, the emotions—greed and confusion and all the others—have destroyed the eternal Veda in the world of men, and so we have become terrified. For when the Veda was destroyed, dharma was lost, too, and we have become the equals of mortals. We used to send rain down, and mortals would rain offerings upwards. But now that their rituals have ceased, we are in danger. Decide what would be best for us in this matter.'

Brahma said to all the gods, 'I will think about what is best; fear no more.' And then he made a work of a hundred thousand chapters, born of his own intelligence, a text describing dharma; and then he made another, for *artha*, about the science of politics, and one about *kama*, for the pursuit of pleasure. Brahma called the group of them, The Triple Path.

Then all the gods went to Vishnu and said, 'Point out the one who alone deserves to be the best of all mortals.' Vishnu thought and then mentally created a glorious son named Virajas. But Virajas did not want the supreme power on earth, for he had set his mind on renunciation. He had a son named Kirtiman, but Kirtiman, too, went away beyond the world of the five senses, and Kirtiman's son, Kardama, also devoted himself to great *tapas* instead of kingship. Kardama had a son named Ananga, a good man who protected his subjects and was adept in the science of wielding the rod of punishment. And Ananga's son, Atibala, understood the science of politics well. But when Atibala became king of the earth he fell under the power of his senses.

Then Sunita, the daughter of Death, gave birth to Vena. But Vena fell into the power of passion and hatred, and he acted against dharma towards his subjects. And so the sages, speaking Vedic verses, killed him with sharp blades of the long, pointed *kusha* grass that they used in ceremonies and that had been purified with Vedic spells. Then the sages churned Vena's right thigh, invoking mantras, and from that thigh a deformed man with a small body was born upon the ground. He had red eyes and dark hair and looked like a pillar that had been burnt. The sages, speaking Vedic verses, said to him, 'Sit down [*nishida*].' And that is how the Nishadas were born, cruel men who live in the mountains and forests, and hundreds and thousands of other barbarians who inhabit the Vindhya mountains.

Then the great sages churned again; this time they churned Vena's right arm, and from it was born a man who had the form of another Indra. He was wearing armour, a girded sword, and a bow and a quiver of arrows, and he had mastered the science of archery. He even knew the Vedas, and the entire science of the rod of punishment. He joined his hands in reverence and said to the great sages, 'A very subtle intelligence, an understanding of the philosophies of dharma and *artha*, has arisen in me. What should I do with it? Advise me about this truly. Whatever you gentlemen will tell me about my duty and its purpose, I will do that, without hesitation.'

The gods and the supreme sages then said to him, 'Wherever dharma is established, attend to it immediately. Be the same to all creatures, disregarding whether you like or dislike them, and cast far away desire and anger and greed and pride. Restrain with your own two arms any man in the world who deviates from dharma. And keep this promise, in what you think and say and do: "I will protect dharma on earth. And I will enforce, without hesitation, the policy of dharma, which is supported by just punishment, and I will never indulge my own will. I will never punish Brahmins. And I will protect the world from any intermarriage of classes whatsoever."'

Prithu then replied to the gods and the sages: 'If the Brahmins will be my allies, let it be so.' 'Let it be so,' the Brahmins said to Prithu, and Shukra, the consigliere of the demons, who was a living storehouse of the Veda, became his priest.[27] The great sage Garga became his astrologer. Prithu created the two bards who sing praises. He made the earth level, for we have heard that before that the earth had been uneven. Vishnu and Indra and Brahma and the gods and sages consecrated him to rule over all creatures as his subjects. The Earth, in person, shared her jewels with him, and so did the Ocean and Himalaya, the supreme mountain. Indra gave him inexhaustible wealth, and great Meru himself, the golden mountain, gave him a golden ornament. Kubera, the master of the Yakshas and Rakshasas, gave him the riches to make him able to maintain dharma and *artha* and *kama*.

Prithu made horses and chariots and elephants and men appear by the tens of thousands, just by thinking of them. There was no old age or starvation, nor any mental agonies or physical diseases. Because of the protection that he secured, no danger ever arose there from creeping serpents or thieves, nor did people fear one another. He milked this earth of its seventeen kinds of grain, and Yakshas and even Rakshasas and Nagas each got whatever they desired. Prithu made this world one in which dharma was supreme. And because he delighted [*ranjita*] all his subjects, they called him 'King' [*raja*]. Because he protected [*tra*] the Brahmins from injury [*kshata*], he was said to be a Kshatriya. Through the king's *tapas*, the lord Vishnu entered him and himself established the fixed rule: 'No one, your majesty, will surpass or offend you.' And therefore the universe bows down before kings as if they were gods.

[12.59]

V. Stories about Kings

The last story in the section on the origin of evil just concluded could well stand as the first story in this section about to begin, for the tale of Vena and Prithu is both a story about the origin of evil *and* a story about the origin of kingship, justifying kingship precisely on the basis of the origin of evil. The stories we are going to consider now focus on various other aspects of the king's duty to combat evil.

The first story insists on what it regards as the very first duty of a king, to punish evil-doers, rather than the duty to protect dharma, that the myth of Prithu had emphasized; ultimately, the two goals are the same, but the tale of Prithu views that royal task positively, and the story of the two brothers views it negatively. The second story, which begins with the murder of a crow, is more complex, spinning a convoluted saga that teaches the king to distinguish between good and bad courtiers and advisers, and to protect the good ones from the bad ones. The third story contests the widely attested assumption—which we have encountered in several other texts—that it is the duty of kings to give gifts to Brahmins. In this rather extreme case, the king is a filicide who engages in witchcraft, and the Brahmins who rightly scorn him are the most famous of all Brahmins, the Seven Sages. Together, these texts suggest that the attitude towards kings in ancient India was morally complex.

26. How a King Cut Off and Restored a Brother's Hands

We have seen that the king's main duty is often said to be to punish. This story is an extreme example of that duty.

The Text

In the course of a long discussion about the virtues and duties of a good king, the sage Vyasa remarked to Yudhishthira, 'It has been heard that King Sudyumna wielded the rod of punishment and achieved great success.' Then Yudhishthira asked, 'What did King Sudyumna do to achieve such great success? I want to hear about that king.' Vyasa replied:

They tell this old story about Shankha and Likhita, two Brahmin brothers who kept strict vows. They had two separate dwellings, charming places on the banks of the Bahuda River, with many trees heavy with fruits and flowers. One day, Likhita came to Shankha's ashram when Shankha happened to have gone out. When Likhita arrived at the ashram, he chanced to knock down some fruits that had just become perfectly ripe. He took them and ate them in good conscience, and just as he was eating them, Shankha returned to the ashram. When Shankha saw his brother eating the fruit, he said, 'Where did you get that fruit? And why are you eating it?' Likhita washed out his mouth and greeted his older brother and smiled and said, 'I got it from here.'

Shankha was filled with sharp anger and said to him, 'When

you took that fruit by yourself you committed a theft. Go to the king and tell him what you've done and say, "Your majesty, you know that, by taking in this way what had not been given, I have become a thief. Therefore you must fulfil your own dharma and quickly give me the punishment for theft."' When he heard this, Likhita, who always kept his vows, went to King Sudyumna.

When King Sudyumna heard from his personal guards that Likhita had arrived, he went on foot with his ministers to greet him. The king met him and said, 'Why have you come? Tell me what you want, my lord, and consider it done.' Likhita replied to Sudyumna, 'Since you have said, "I promise I will do it," you should listen and then do it. Your majesty, I ate fruit that my older brother had not given me. Punish me for that without delay.' Sudyumna said, 'If you know that the king has the authority to punish, then you know that he can also pardon. You have been pardoned, for your karma is pure and you have undertaken great vows. Tell me, what wishes other than this can I fulfil for you? I will do what you say.'

Though Likhita was pleased by the king's words, he did not choose any boon but the boon of being punished. Then the king had Likhita's two hands cut off, and Likhita, enduring his punishment in great physical pain, left. He went to his brother Shankha and said, 'You should forgive me, for I have been punished for my stupidity.' Shankha said, 'I am not angry with you, nor have you done me any harm. But you violated dharma, and this was your restoration for that. Go quickly now to the Bahuda River and satisfy the gods and the ancestors and the sages according to the rituals, and do not set your mind on the violation of dharma.'

Likhita went and plunged into the auspicious river Bahuda and began the water rituals. Then his two hands appeared, like two lotuses born from the water. Amazed, he showed his two hands to his brother. Shankha said, 'This was done through my *tapas*. Let there be no doubt about this: it was fated to happen.' Likhita said, 'Why did you not purify me sooner? Since your *tapas* has such power.' Shankha said, 'I had to do it like this, for I am not the one responsible for punishing you. The king has been purified, together with his ancestors, and so have you.'

That king became preeminent and supremely successful because of this deed. This is the dharma of Kshatriyas, to protect their subjects—through punishment.

[12.24]

27. How the King of Kosala Rewarded the Man Whose Crow was Murdered

The themes of violence and retributive punishment prevail here too, but now embedded in a more elaborate narrative.

The Text

Bhishma said to Yudhishthira, 'Those who would raid the king's treasury get together and together attack the person who guards the king's treasury; and if that person is not protected, he is destroyed. On that subject, they tell this old story about what the sage Kalakavrikshiya said to the King of Kosala.'

When Kshemadarshin had become king of the Kosalas, the Brahmin sage Kalakavrikshiya came to him; so we have heard. Kalakavrikshiya had put a crow in a cage and wandered around Kshemadarshin's territory, time and again, observing the behaviour of the people, particularly of those in the service of the king. 'I study the knowledge of crows,' he said, 'for my crows advise me about what will happen, what has happened, and what is happening right now.' Wandering about the kingdom, he inquired among many men about the misdeeds of all the people employed by the king. He found out what was being undertaken everywhere in the kingdom and all the misdeeds of the king's employees, in one place and another. Taking his crow with him, Kalakavrikshiya went to see Kshemadarshin the king of Kosala and said, 'I know everything.' He went up to a richly adorned minister of the king and said, because of what the crow had said, 'You did this, in this place. This person and that person know that you have stolen from the king's treasury.' And that man understood immediately, 'This is what that crow has reported.' Kalakavrikshiya spoke in this way to others, too, who had stolen from the king's treasury. And never was anything that he was heard to report proven not to have been done.

All the king's servants whom he had thwarted attacked him in the night when he was asleep, but they murdered only his crow. In the morning, seeing his crow shattered by an arrow in his cage, Kalakavrikshiya said to Kshemadarshin, 'Your majesty, I ask you for protection, for safe conduct, for you are the ruler. If I have your permission, I would speak words that are for the welfare of your city. I am deeply unhappy for the sake of my friend the king, and have come with wholehearted devotion, as one who would say to you, because he cannot bear to put up with it, "This person is stealing your property." I hope to rouse a friend, as a charioteer rouses a good horse, and because I want to do what is best for you, I am motivated by great righteous anger. A wise person who wishes to rule and constantly strives to succeed should always put up with that sort of friend.' The king replied to him, 'Whatever you say to me, how could I not forgive it, wishing as I do for my own welfare? Brahmin, I promise you, say whatever you wish. For I will do what you say, no matter what you say to me.'

Kalakavrikshiya said, 'My crow has been sent to his death. I don't think you deserve to be reproached for this, nor do those who hold you dear. But you must tell the difference between those who wish you well and those who do not; do not think that this cannot be known. The people who live in your house and care only for what they can get, who do not wish your people to prosper—people like that have targeted me. They hope to get the kingdom by destroying you. But only by allying themselves with those who are your intimates will they succeed, not otherwise. Because I fear them, your majesty, I will go to another ashram. For my crow was brought down by an arrow that they aimed at me. My crow was sent to the house of Yama, god of the dead, as a cryptic signal to me; I saw this through my gaze made farsighted by *tapas*. Using the crow as a fish-hook, I have taken you across this river filled with many crocodiles, alligators and sharks.

'Just as a great creeper attaches itself to a great tree and grows great, and completely surrounds the tree and grows beyond it, and then a terrible forest fire uses it for tinder and burns the tree—your ministers are just like that, your majesty. Purge them! You have made them and you have protected them, your majesty. Now they disdain you and want to kill someone dear to you, someone who wants to find out the true nature of the king by living with him, someone who lives in fear and suspicion, constantly guarding against making a careless mistake, like living in a house with a snake inside it, or in a home with the wife of a powerful man.

'Has the king conquered his senses? Has he conquered his

inner emotions? Is the king dear to his people? And are his subjects dear to the king? Wanting to know this, I came here to you. You pleased me, your majesty, like food for a starving man. But your ministers do not please me, like water for a man who is not thirsty. Knowing that I was working for your benefit, they accused me of transgressions. There is no other reason for this; I bear them no malice, but that is the offence that they have committed against me. For one should always fear an enemy who has been only partly wounded, like a snake with a broken back.'

The king said, 'Best of Brahmins, live on longer in my house, served with lavish accommodations and honoured by great reverence. Those who do not like you will not live in my house. For you are the one who will know what is to be done now, immediately. Judging how to punish those who have done evil, and how to reward what is done well, good sir, guide me so that I may do what is best.' Kalakavrikshiya replied, 'Disregarding this one particular crime [killing the crow], weaken them one by one, and then, when you have understood each motive, kill one man after another. For when many men have committed the same crime, they might crush people who are thorns in their sides. I am telling you this, your majesty, because I fear that your secret counsel might be violated. We Brahmins punish mildly and are inclined to compassion. I wish for your welfare, and that of your enemies, as I wish for my own. I am known as the sage Kalakavrikshiya. I was the friend of your father and am your friend; I am an honourable person who keeps his promises. Now that your kingdom, which your father established, is in trouble, I forsook all pleasures and generated *tapas*. I am saying this out of my affection for you, in the hope that you may not go on making mistakes. Now that you have by chance obtained this kingdom, if you considered the two alternatives, for its happiness or misery, how can you have been so careless in establishing the ministers for the kingdom?'

Then great joy arose once more in the king's family, when Kalakavrikshiya was made the royal chaplain. Putting the earth under a single umbrella for the glorious king of Kosala, Kalakavrikshiya sacrificed with the greatest sacrificial rituals. Taking heed of the sage's words for his welfare, and doing just what Kalakavrikshiya had said to do, the king of Kosala governed the earth.

[12.83]

28. How the Seven Sages Refused a Gift from a King

The stories we have considered so far (all, of course, written by Brahmins), assume that kings respect and support Brahmins, in return for which, Brahmins grant kings political supremacy. But there is also another line of argument in these texts that exalts Brahmins at the expense of kings. The following story is one of that sort.

The Seven Sages, a group of seven particularly holy Brahmins, encounter the evil King Shaibya, who has sacrificed his son and now attempts, in vain, first to corrupt and then to destroy the Seven Sages through his agent, a witch named Yatudhani ('Womb of Demons'). The sages are saved by Shunahsakha, a wandering magician who is revealed, at the end, to be a god in disguise, and not just any god, but Indra himself—Indra who so often appears in disguise to foil Brahmins (or to seduce their wives). There is surely an irony in the choice of Indra, a god who so frequently violates dharma and cuckolds Brahmins, as the one to save the ultimate Brahmin sages from an evil king and to teach them a lesson about dharma.

The plot turns upon the witch's attempt to learn the names of the Seven Sages, which she needs in order to put a spell upon them, as the wicked king Shaibya has commanded her to do. The sages, under the protection and guidance of Shunahsakha, answer with punning versions of their names, and so they fool the witch and foil the king. (The puns are quite clever in Sanskrit, but, as they don't work well in English, I have just translated the first one of the seven.)

The immediate issue that precipitates the story is the rule that a Brahmin may lose merit if he receives a gift from someone evil, particularly (as the story goes on to argue) from a king—any king, apparently (a direct contradiction of the more general praise of kings generous to Brahmins, which we have observed in several stories), but especially one who has, to take a case at random, murdered his son.

The Text

Yudhishthira asked, 'People give many different sorts of gifts to Brahmins. What is the connection between the donor and the recipient?' Bhishma replied, 'A Brahmin may receive a gift from a person who is virtuous as well as from one who is not virtuous. There is little fault if the donor has good qualities; but if he has no good quality, the recipient loses merit. In this connection they tell this ancient story about a conversation between the Seven Sages and King Shaibya.'

The Seven Sages—Atri, Bharadvaja, Gautama, Jamadagni, Kashyapa, Vasishtha, and Vishvamitra—together with the virtuous Arundhati, Vasishtha's wife, all were served by a servant girl named Ganda, whose husband was a Shudra named

Pashusakha. Once upon a time, as they were all engaged in *tapas*, they wandered over the earth, hoping to win the eternal world through meditation.

Now, a great drought arose, in which the world, suffering from hunger, was down to its last life's breaths.

Sometime earlier, King Shaibya had offered a sacrifice in which his own son was sacrificed and given as the payment to the sacrificial priests. The boy, who had a short lifespan, went to his appointed end. Now the Seven Sages, tormented by hunger, sat around the dead boy who had been sacrificed. When they saw that there was no breath of life in him, they began to cook him on a pan. As there was nothing to eat in the world of mortals, and as they wished to save their own lives, the sages resorted to this painful course of action, to get food.

Then King Shaibya, wandering about, saw them on the road, suffering as they cooked. Shaibya said, 'Don't eat something that should not be eaten! What can I offer you to sustain you? Accepting a gift can save you. Accept it for your nourishment. I love a Brahmin who asks me for something. What can I give you? I will tell you what wealth I have. Let me give you rice and barley, delicious juices, and any precious item that is hard to get.' The sages said, 'Your majesty, receiving a gift from a king may taste like honey but it is like poison. Knowing this, why are you tempting us? Kshatriyas depend on Brahmins as they depend on deities. The *tapas* that a Brahmin creates here in just one single day would be burnt up as if by a forest fire, were he to receive anything from a king. May you always have the good fortune that is won by giving, your majesty, but give it all to those who seek it.' And having said that, they went away. The meat that those wise men had put on the fire remained entirely uncooked. They all left it and went into the woods, hoping to find food.

The king then urged his ministers to go to the forest, where they picked some figs and began to give them away as gifts. Their servants put gold inside some of the figs and ran after the sages to get them to accept them. But Atri, realizing, 'They are heavy! And so we must not accept them,' said, 'We are not fools or idiots. We know that these are made of gold; we are wide awake. For whatever is accepted here, however sweet, will give rise to bitterness in the world hereafter. This food should absolutely not be accepted by anyone who wishes for happiness here and after death.'

One by one each of the other six sages, and Arundhati, and Ganda and Pashusakha, refused the figs and the gold. The sages said, 'Let the king prosper by giving to his own subjects these stuffed fruits that you have offered to us.' And then the sages left the fruits with the gold inside, thus maintaining their vows, and they all went somewhere else. The ministers said to the king, 'They suspected a trick and refused these fruits and went somewhere else, your majesty.'

When Shaibya heard his servants' report, he became furious. He went home. To take revenge on all of them, he undertook a terrible vow and offered oblations into the sacred fire, while chanting mantras. A terrifying witch, like the night of doomsday, arose out of the fire, and Shaibya named her Yatudhani. The witch joined her hands in reverence and approached King Shaibya and said, 'What shall I do?' Shaibya said, 'Get hold of the minds of the Seven Sages and Arundhati and their male servant and female servant. Find out their names so that you can destroy them all. And when they have all been destroyed, go wherever you wish.' The witch promised, 'Yes!' and went to the forest where the great sages, led by Atri, were wandering about, eating fruits and roots. There the sages saw the sage Shunahsakha; he had a well-fleshed body, with plump shoulders and hands and feet and face and stomach. When Arundhati saw him with all his well-fleshed limbs, she said to the sages, 'You will never be like that!'

Vasishtha said, 'Shunahsakha is plump because, unlike us, his oblation fire does not lack oblations of butter; he makes oblations into his fire, morning and evening.' And each of the other sages cited another reason, another virtue, that kept Shunahsakha plump: Atri: 'Shunahsakha is plump because he is not hungry, and, unlike us, he still has his learning.' Vishvamitra: 'Shunahsakha is plump because he is not lazy, obsessed with hunger, and foolish, like us, nor is his knowledge of the ancient texts tired out like an old bull, as ours is.' Jamadagni: 'Shunahsakha is plump because he doesn't have to think all the time about the yearly supply of food and kindling, as we do.' Kashyapa: 'Shunahsakha is plump because he doesn't have brothers who keep begging, "Give! Give!"' Bharadvaja: 'Shunahsakha is plump because he is not saddened by his wife's accusations and recriminations.' Gautama: 'Shunahsakha is plump because he is not wearing just one deer hide that's three years old.'

When Shunahsakha saw those great sages, he approached them in a polite manner and touched their hands. They told one another about their wandering in the forest, how their activity was hindered by their hunger, and so they set out together. With one mind about what had to be done, they roamed about in the forests, taking up roots and picking fruits.

One day, they saw a beautiful lotus pond, full of clear water covered with lotus petals the colour of lapis lazuli, surrounded by dense trees, shining with flowers shaped like the rising sun, with all sorts of birds that lived on the water. The pond had no mud, was not fed by a river, and had just a single path of access with good steps for bathing. But the witch named Yatudhani, in the employ of King Shaibya, had disguised her face and guarded that lotus pond. The great sages, with Shunahsakha, all went to the lotus pond that the witch guarded, to get lotus filaments to eat. When the sages saw Yatudhani (with her disguised face) standing on the bank of the lotus pond, they said to her, 'Who are you, standing alone on the bank of this lotus pond, and for what purpose and for whose sake? What do you wish to do? Tell us.' Yatudhani said, 'I am who I am, and I should never be questioned about it. Know that I am the protectress of the lotus pond.' The sages said, 'We are all suffering from hunger, and we have nothing else. With your permission, good lady, let us all gather lotus filaments.'

Yatudhani said, 'Take as many lotus filaments as you like from here, on this condition: one by one, tell me your names, and then take the filaments without delay.' But Atri realized that Yatudhani was a witch who wished to kill the sages, and though he was overcome by hunger, he said, 'I study at night [*ratri*] that is not a night [*a-ratri*] for three [*tri*] days, and so my name is not a night [*a-ratri*] but not-three [*a-tri*].' Yatudhani said, 'The name you have explained to me in this way is hard for me to understand. But go down into the lotus pond.' Then Vasishtha, Kashyapa, Bharadvaja, Gautama, Vishvamitra, Jamadagni, Arundhati, Ganda, and Pashusakha similarly riddled on their names, one by one, and Yatudhani let them go down into the lotus pond.

Then Shunahsakha ['Friend of a Dog'] said, 'I cannot say my name as these people have said theirs. But understand that I am the friend of those who are friends of dogs.' Yatudhani said, 'Your name as you have said it is not clear, for you speak with ambiguity. Therefore, tell me your name again now.' Shunahsakha said, 'I told you my name several times, but you did not get it. Therefore, once you have been struck by my triple staff, turn to ashes without delay.' When she was struck on the head with that stick that was like the staff of a Brahmin, the witch fell on the ground and was reduced to ashes. And when Shunahsakha had killed the immensely powerful Yatudhani, he propped up his staff on the ground and sat down on the grass.

Then all the sages collected all the flowers and lotus filaments that they wanted and came out of the water, rejoicing. But as they were overcome by great exhaustion, they threw the filaments down on the bank of the lotus pond in bundles and refreshed themselves by going back into the water. And when they all came up out of the water again, they did not see the lotus filaments. The sages said: 'What cruel villain took away the lotus filaments from us when we were overcome by hunger and looking forward to our food?' They suspected and questioned one another, and then they all said, 'Let us swear an oath.' 'Agreed!' they all said, for they were hungry and exhausted, and so they began to swear their oaths:

Atri said, 'Let the person who stole the lotus filaments touch a cow with his feet and piss facing the sun; and let him study texts that should not be studied.' Each of the others then swore that the person who stole the lotus filaments would commit some similar terrible breach of dharma. Arundhati and Ganda and Pashusakha swore too.

But Shunahsakha said, 'Let the person who stole the lotus filaments give his daughter to a sacrificial priest, or one who knows the verses and is chaste; let him study the Vedas.' The sages said: 'This curse that you have made is what Brahmins wish for. You are the one who has stolen all our lotus filaments.' Shunahsakha said, 'What you said when you had performed your rituals and could not see the food that you had set down—that is all true, not false. I stole the lotus filaments. See here these lotus filaments that I made disappear. I did it to test you. I came here to protect all of you. For this Yatudhani was a very angry witch who was born out of fire to harm you; she hated you and was employed by King Shaibya; and I killed her. That is why I came here. Know that I am Indra. Because you have no greed, you have won the undying worlds that everyone wishes for. Stand up! Go quickly from here and find those worlds.'

The great sages were delighted and said 'Yes!' to Indra. And all of them went to heaven with him. In this way, those great men who had suffered terrible hunger enjoyed many sorts of pleasures. As they did not submit to greed, they won heaven. And so, in all circumstances, a man must reject greed. Lack of greed is known to be the supreme dharma.

[13.94–5]

VI. Stories about Indra, King of the Gods

The final story in the previous section about kings—a story that also turned out to be, among other things, a story about Indra, king of the gods—forms a bridge to this section. We have encountered Indra as an often disreputable bit player in a number of other stories before now, but in the following section, he is—though still significantly flawed—the main protagonist.

The story of Indra's fight against the demon/serpent Vritra is one of the oldest and most-retold myths in India. It begins in the Veda. Indeed, it begins long before that, in the Indo-European mythology about Indra and his cousins Zeus and Jupiter and Wotan: sky gods, rain gods, sexual predators and kings of the gods, all with their dragon-killing thunderbolt weapons. And this mythology goes on right through to the present day. Several versions of Indra's killing of the demons Vritra, Vishvarupa, and Nahusha appear in this part of the *Mahabharata*.

The fact that Vritra is both a Brahmin and a demon (an *asura*, by definition the enemy of the gods, the *suras* or *devas*) means that Indra must kill him even though he must then atone for the sin of Brahminicide, Brahmin-killing—a sin that, you will not be surprised to learn, the Brahmin authors of our text regard as the very most serious of all evil actions. This problem is exacerbated by the well-known fact (which we have encountered in a number of texts in this collection) that Indra is notorious for his violence and for his disregard for dharma, particularly (through his invention of adultery and his frequent indulgence in it) the dharma of marriage. The conflict between Indra and

Vritra is therefore not simply another dragon-slayer myth but an expression of a deep conflict between the ideals of kingship and the ideals of Brahminhood. I have included two rather different versions of the Indra–Vritra conflict, the first fairly straightforward, the second more metaphysical.

Indra's battle with Vishvarupa also involves the Brahmin–Kshatriya conflict, as Vishvarupa is, though a demon, a sacrificial priest. But Indra's conflict with Nahusha is more banal: they are fighting over Indra's wife, Shachi, who is not simply a female but the very essence of power (which is what *shachi* means in Sanskrit). Indra's encounter with Uttanka (yet another Brahmin) demonstrates just how trivial, jealous, and vulgar the king of the gods can be—perhaps a Brahminical joke at the expense of the Kshatriyas.

29. How Indra Killed Vritra and Suffered from Brahminicide

The simultaneously demonic and Brahminic status of Vritra in the *Mahabharata*, pitted against the simultaneously godlike and vice-ridden nature of Indra, king of the gods, expresses important aspects of the shifting balance of power and virtue between Brahmins and kings. Back in the Veda, the equine Indra triumphed over the serpentine dragon Vritra and no questions were asked; there was dancing in the streets. But in later texts, such as the *Mahabharata*, Indra can kill the Brahminic Vritra only with the help of the post-Vedic gods Shiva and Vishnu, and even then, Indra pays dearly for his Pyrrhic victory.

The Text

Yudhishthira said, 'I beg you to dispel this doubt that I'm asking about: How did Indra conquer Vritra? Tell me in great detail how the battle took place, for I am most curious about it.' Bhishma said:

Once upon a time, Indra set forth on his chariot, with the hosts of gods, and he saw Vritra standing in front of him, like a mountain, five hundred leagues high and three hundred leagues wide. When the gods saw Vritra like that, they were terrified. And when Indra saw Vritra's enormous form, he was immediately so frightened that his thighs trembled.

All the gods and demons made a tremendous noise with their musical instruments. But when Vritra saw Indra coming at him, he was not afraid or upset at all; he didn't care. Then a terrifying battle for the triple world took place between Indra and Vritra. With swords, battle-axes, tridents, spears, clubs, various sorts of stones, bows, knives, flaming missiles—all was crowded confusion in the armies of the gods and the demons.

From his mountain, Vritra hurled down on Indra a rain of boulders that filled the air. The gods, infuriated by this torrent of weapons, repelled the boulders that Vritra had sent forth in the battle. But Vritra, who had not only great strength but great magic, deluded Indra with his magic weapons from all sides. Confusion overcame Indra when Vritra had attacked him, but the great Brahmin sage Vasishtha, in another chariot, awakened Indra to his senses, saying, 'You are the greatest of the gods, empowered by all the might of the triple worlds. How can you lose heart like this? Brahma is here, and Vishnu and Shiva, and all the great sages. Do not be faint-hearted, like some other sort of god. Make up your noble mind to fight and conquer your enemy.' In this way, Vasishtha awakened Indra's great power and energy. And so Indra, regaining his senses, yoked himself with his great yoga and dispelled Vritra's magic.

Then Brihaspati and the great sages, seeing Vritra's courage and prowess, went to Shiva and spoke to him about the need to destroy Vritra for the sake of the worlds. The fiery energy of Shiva became fever [*jvara*] and entered Vritra, the supreme and horrible demon. And Vishnu, taking pleasure in the protection of the worlds, entered Indra's thunderbolt. Then Brihaspati and Vasishtha and all the supreme sages approached Indra. Together they honoured Indra and, with one mind, said, 'Kill Vritra.'

Shiva said, 'Indra, this Vritra is cloaked in great power. As he has strong magic and is deeply learned, he can go everywhere. Do not despise him! He is the greatest of the demons and hard even for the master of the entire triple world to conquer. But you must kill him by engaging in yoga. For he has generated *tapas* for sixty thousand years to get his power, and Brahma granted him his boon: he has the greatness of yogis, and their magic power, and their strength and supreme energy. But once this energy of mine, in the form of fever, has gotten inside Vritra, even you can kill him with your thunderbolt.' Indra said, 'By your favour, and right under your eyes, I will take my thunderbolt and kill this demon who is so hard to attack.'

When the fever sent by Shiva had permeated the great demon, a great shout of joy arose among the gods and sages, who praised Indra and urged him on. Big drums, little drums, noisy conch shells, and tambourines resounded by the thousands. In a single moment, all the demons lost their memory and their understanding.

The fever pervaded Vritra everywhere, and these signs appeared on his body: His mouth was aflame and gruesome, and he became extremely pale. His limbs trembled greatly, and his breathing was heavy. The hair on his body stood sharply on end, and he sighed deeply. His memory fell out of his mouth in the form of a most horrible and inauspicious jackal, and blazing meteors fell down his sides. Vultures, herons and cranes circled over Vritra excitedly, emitting most horrible cries.

As the battle raged, Indra, mounted on his chariot, raised up his thunderbolt in his hand and looked right at the demon. Vishnu pervaded the thunderbolt. The great demon let out an inhuman roar and yawned, for he was filled with the sharp fever. And as Vritra was yawning, Indra let loose his thunderbolt. That enormously powerful thunderbolt, like the fire of doomsday, immediately fell into the great body of the demon. Then a tremendous roar arose again on all sides, as the gods saw that Vritra had been killed. And when Indra had killed Vritra with the thunderbolt, he entered heaven.

But then the incarnation of Brahminicide [*brahmahatya*], the terror of the worlds, came out of Vritra's body. Terrifying and deformed, horrible and fierce, she had a gaping mouthful of teeth and was dark and tawny; her hair was dishevelled, and her eyes were horrible. She was emaciated and dripping with blood, and she wore a garland of skulls and clothes made of skins. As soon as she came out of Vritra, in that terrifying form, she began to hunt for Indra.

When the fear of Brahminicide arose in Indra, he hid in the middle of the stalk of a lotus for many years. But after a while, Indra the Killer of Vritra came out and headed for heaven. Seeing Indra as he was coming out of the lotus stalk, Brahminicide grabbed him by the neck and held him fast. For she had followed him unrelentingly and finally had caught him. Indra made a great effort to shake her off but was unable to do it. With her still firmly grabbing him by the neck, Indra went to Brahma and honoured him just by bowing his head. And when Brahma realized that Indra had been seized by Brahminicide, he spoke to Brahminicide in a honeyed voice, trying to conciliate her: 'Do me a favour, good lady, and let Indra go free. Tell me what I can do for you today. What desire of yours do you wish to have fulfilled here?'

Brahminicide said, 'If you, the maker of the triple worlds, are pleased, then I regard myself as fulfilled. For you created the great moral law and promulgated it in order to protect the worlds. If you are pleased, I will go away from Indra. But give me a place to live.' 'Yes!' said Brahma to Brahminicide. And this is how Brahma expelled Brahminicide from Indra:

Brahma thought of Fire, who came to him and said: 'I have arrived. Tell me what is to be done.' Brahma said, 'I will divide this Brahminicide into four parts to free Indra from it today.

Receive one quarter of it from me.' Fire said, 'How will there be an end to it, so that I can be free? Think about this. I want to know this truly.' Brahma said, 'When any human man who approaches you when you are aflame fails to sacrifice seeds and herbs and juices into the fire, this Brahminicide will quickly enter into him and will stay right there. And so you may stop worrying.' Fire agreed to this promise from Brahma, and so it was.

Then Brahma summoned the trees, herbs and grasses and made the same proposal to them. But the trees, herbs and grasses were just as disturbed as Fire had been, and they said to Brahma, 'What end will there be to the Brahminicide that has been placed in us? You should not wound us even more when we are already wounded by our very nature. For we always have to bear heat and cold and wind-driven rain, and being cut down and chopped up, and now by your command we will get this Brahminicide. You ought to think of a release for us!' Brahma said, 'When any man, in his delusion, cuts you down and chops you up on the lunar holy days, this Brahminicide will follow him.' When the trees and herbs and grasses heard this, they honoured Brahma and went quickly back whence they had come.

Then Brahma summoned the Apsarases and tried to conciliate them with honeyed words: 'Fine ladies, this Brahminicide has come from Indra. Let me ask you to accept a quarter of it.' The Apsarases said, 'We have decided to take it, as you command. But you must think of a way of releasing us from this agreement.' Brahma said, 'If any man has sex with women who are menstruating, this fever of the mind will quickly enter him and leave you.' 'Agreed,' said the host of Apsarases, delighted, and they went back to their own places, rejoicing.

Then Brahma thought again and mentally summoned the waters, and as soon as they were thought of, they came there. They all bowed low to Brahma and said, 'We have all come here by your command. Tell us what to do.' Brahma said: 'This Brahminicide has come from Vritra and is terrifying Indra. You must receive a quarter of it.' The waters said, 'Let it be just as you are telling us. But you should think of some way for us to be released from this agreement. Who other than you could grant us the favour of setting us free from this tight spot?' Brahma said, 'If any man, deluded in his wits, thinks, "The waters are trivial," and releases phlegm or urine or faeces into you, this Brahminicide will quickly enter him and settle down right there. And in this way your release will come about. I am telling you the truth.'

And so Brahminicide left Indra and, by Brahma's command, went to the designated places. And that is how Brahminicide came to Indra, who, on the advice of Brahma, performed a horse sacrifice and was purified. Regaining his glory, Indra killed his enemies by the thousands, and rejoiced.

[12.272]

30. How Indra Killed Vishvarupa with the Bones of Dadhicha

Indra's other great enemy is Vishvarupa, whom this text regards as the progenitor of Vritra. This too is a retold Vedic story with a Vedic background lineage: Vishvarupa's father was Tvashtri, the artisan of the gods, the Indian Hephaestus/Vulcan, but Vishvarupa's mother was the sister of a demon.

The Text

King Janamejaya asked the bard about the superiority of Brahmins, and the bard told him this story.

Vishvarupa, the three-headed son of Tvashtri, was the sacrificial priest of the gods, but he was a nephew of the demons, for his mother's brother was a demon. In public he gave the greater share of the sacrifice to the gods, but privately he gave a small share to the demons. The demons asked a favour from their sister, Vishvarupa's mother: 'Sister, this son of yours, Tvashtri's son Vishvarupa, is the sacrificial priest of the gods. Publicly he has been giving the greater portion to the gods, but privately just a small portion to us. And so the gods are growing greater and we are growing weaker. Now, you should control him in such a way that he will share the whole sacrifice with us.' So Vishvarupa's mother went to him and said, 'My son, why are you making the other side thrive and destroying your mother's side? You should not act like this.'

Vishvarupa, thinking that one should not disobey a mother's words, engaged in extreme *tapas* to increase the power of his mother's family. To make him break his vow, Indra employed many gorgeous Apsarases. When Vishvarupa saw them, his mind was shaken, and very soon he became attracted to those Apsarases. And knowing that he was attached to them, the Apsarases said, 'Let's go back where we came from.' Vishvarupa said to them, 'Where will you go? As long as you stay with me, you will do very well.' They said to him, 'We are Apsarases, women of the gods. In the past, we were married to Indra.' Then Vishvarupa said to them, 'From this very day, the gods and Indra will no longer exist.' And then he muttered some mantras, and by those mantras he grew great. With one of his three mouths, he drank all the Soma that had been offered up in the sacrifices by the Brahmins performing all the rituals in all the worlds; with another mouth he drank the waters; and with the third mouth he began to eat the gods and Indra.

When Indra saw that Vishvarupa was growing stronger in all his limbs by drinking the Soma, he became worried. He went with the gods to Brahma and said, 'Vishvarupa is drinking the Soma that has been offered in all the sacrifices. We now have no share at all. The faction of the demons is growing stronger and greater while we are growing weaker and smaller. You should do what is best for us, and right away.' Brahma said, 'The sage Dadhicha is generating great *tapas*. Ask him to do a favour for you by giving up his body. And make a thunderbolt with his bones.'

The gods, with Indra, went where Dadhicha was generating *tapas* and went up to him and said, 'We hope your *tapas* is going well, and with no obstacles.' Dadhicha said to them, 'Welcome! What has to be done for you? Tell me and I will do it.' They said to him, 'You must give up your body for the sake of the welfare of the worlds.' Then Dadhicha, not at all bothered, said, 'So be it,' for he was a great yogi to whom happiness and misery were the same. And he collected his *atman* and abandoned his body.

Then Brahma gathered Dadhicha's bones together and made a thunderbolt. And with that unbreakable and irresistible thunderbolt, made out of the bones of a Brahmin and pervaded by Vishnu, Indra killed Vishvarupa and cut off his three heads.

Immediately after that, they churned the limbs of Vishvarupa and Vritra was born, and Indra killed him.

[12.329c]

31. How Nahusha Usurped Indra's Throne

In addition to the problems that Indra has with the two major demons, Vritra and Vishvarupa, he also has to deal with miscellaneous minor characters who threaten not only the security of the universe but the security of Indra's own marriage. Here, as usual, after killing Vritra, Indra must rid himself of Brahminicide, but this time that episode is dealt with in just a few lines. For now the real problem lies elsewhere, with the threat to Indra's wife, whose name is, appropriately, Shachi, a Sanskrit word for 'power'.

The Text

The bard continues to explain the superiority of Brahmins to King Janamejaya, by telling him another story about Indra.

After Indra had killed Vishvarupa and Vritra, he was afraid because he had killed two Brahmins, and so he abandoned his dominion as king of the gods and went into a lotus stalk growing in the cool waters of Lake Manasa. He had used his yogic powers to become very small, and then he entered the fibres of the lotus.

Now, when Indra had been destroyed by his terror of Brahminicide, the universe was without a ruler. Passion and darkness entered the gods. The great sages did not chant the mantras, and Rakshasas appeared everywhere. The Veda was put aside. The worlds, without an Indra, without a king of the gods, were subject to violence.

And so the gods and sages consecrated King Nahusha as king of the gods. Nahusha, with five hundred blazing stars on his forehead, stole everyone's energy and began to rule the triple world. The worlds regained their natural form and became stable. But then Nahusha said, 'I have gotten everything that Indra used to enjoy, except his wife, Shachi.' He went to Shachi and said to her, 'Lovely lady, I am now the Indra of the gods. Come to bed with me.' Shachi replied to him, 'You are by nature devoted to dharma, and you were born in the lunar royal lineage. You should not rape another man's wife.'

Nahusha replied to her, 'I have attained Indra's position, and I have taken all the jewels of Indra's kingdom. There is no violation of dharma at all in this. For Indra used to enjoy you.' She said to him, 'There is a certain vow that I have not concluded. When it has been fulfilled, I will come to you, after a few days.' And Nahusha left.

Then Shachi was miserable, longing for a sight of her husband and gripped by fear of Nahusha. She went to Brihaspati, and as soon as he saw that she had arrived, Brihaspati meditated and realized that her husband's goals were her top priority. So he said, 'Fortified by your marriage vow and by your *tapas*, seek a boon from the goddess called "The Listener" [*upashruti*],[28] and she will show you your Indra.'

And so Shachi undertook a great vow and said mantras to invoke the Listener, a goddess who grants boons. The Listener came to Shachi and said to her, 'You have summoned me and here I am. What favour can I do for you?' Shachi bowed to her with her head and said, 'Goddess, please show me my husband.' And so the goddess led Shachi to Lake Manasa, and there she showed her Indra inside the filament of the lotus.

When Indra saw his wife so thin and pale, he began to worry: 'Oh dear! What a great calamity has befallen me today. For this woman, suffering miserably, has followed me in my destruction.' And Indra said to her, 'How are you doing?' and she said to him, 'Nahusha is summoning me. I have gotten him to give me some time.' Indra said to her, 'Go. Say to Nahusha,

"You should carry me off on a carriage never seen before, one that is yoked to sages. For I have ridden on Indra's great carriages, that thrilled my heart. You should drive me on a different one."' Delighted, she left. And Indra went back once again inside the lotus filament.

When Nahusha saw that Shachi had returned, he said to her, 'The time is up.' And Shachi replied to him as Indra had told her to do. So Nahusha yoked the Seven Sages to a chariot and mounted it and came to Shachi.

The powerful sage Agastya saw Nahusha mistreating those seven great sages, and then Nahusha touched Agastya with his feet. At this, Agastya said to Nahusha, 'Since you have done what is not to be done, you evil creature, fall to the earth. Become a serpent, for as long as the earth and the mountains stand.' And even while the great sage was speaking, Nahusha fell from that chariot and from heaven.

But now the triple world was once again without an Indra. And so the gods and sages sought refuge with Vishnu, because they needed an Indra. They said to him, 'Lord, you should save Indra, who has been overcome by Brahminicide.' Then Vishnu, always inclined to grant a boon, said to them, 'Let Indra sacrifice with a horse sacrifice dedicated to Vishnu. In that way he will regain his own position.'

But then, when the gods and sages still could not see Indra, they said to Shachi, 'Go, good lady, to Indra and bring him here.' She went back to that lake, and Indra rose out of it and went to Brihaspati. Brihaspati performed a great horse sacrifice for Indra, releasing the dappled sacrificial stallion to wander for a year and then sacrificing him, and in that way, Indra regained his own place. Then the gods and sages praised the king of the gods, who was established in heaven, free of moral stain. And

Indra divided Brahminicide into four parts, among women, fire, trees and cows.[29] In this way, Indra, enlarged by the power of a Brahmin's energy, killed his enemies and regained his own place.

[12.329]

32. How Indra Killed Vritra

This version of the story is not so much a battle story as a metaphysical meditation on the great myth.

The Text

When Krishna knew that King Yudhishthira was depressed in mind and heart, because his friends and relatives had been killed; that he was like a sun in eclipse, like a smoking fire; he began to speak to Yudhishthira to console him. Krishna said: 'The whole realm of death is crooked, and the realm of the godhead is straight. What good can weeping do? You have not perfected your karma, nor have you conquered your enemies. How is it that you do not understand that the enemy is your self, dwelling in your body? On this subject I will explain to you how the fight took place between Indra and Vritra.'

Once upon a time, the earth was pervaded by the demonic serpent Vritra, and when Indra saw this, and saw that the essence of the earth's perfume had been stolen, and that a bad smell had arisen as a result, he became furious, and in his fury he hurled his terrible thunderbolt at Vritra. When Vritra, lurking in the earth, was struck by that thunderbolt, he immediately entered the waters and took away their essence, the essence of taste. Then, Indra, furious, hurled his thunderbolt at Vritra again, and when the thunderbolt struck Vritra in the water, he immediately entered the light and took away its essence, the essence of form. Then Indra, furious, hurled his thunderbolt at Vritra again. Struck very hard by the thunderbolt, Vritra entered the wind and took away its essence, the essence of touch. Again Indra, furious, hurled his thunderbolt at him, and now Vritra fled to space and took away its essence, the essence of sound.

Then Indra, furious, hurled his thunderbolt yet again at Vritra. Struck by the thunderbolt, this time Vritra immediately entered Indra and took away *his* essence. A great coma overcame Indra when Vritra had grabbed him, and the sage Vasishtha awakened Indra from that coma by means of a Vedic chant. Then Indra killed Vritra—who was within his body—by means of an invisible thunderbolt; this is what we have heard about that. Indra proclaimed this secret among the great seers, and the seers proclaimed it to me.

Learn it, your majesty.

[14.11]

33. How Indra Tricked Uttanka into Rejecting the Soma

Indra in this story has lost his Vedic splendour; indeed, by this time he has sunk so low that he takes the form of a Dalit. So art the mighty fallen!

We have already met the sage Uttanka in the episode in which Ahalya sends him to the underworld to get her earrings. In that story, Uttanka was involved with the anus of a horse, a Kshatriya animal; here he is involved with the penis of what appears to be a low-caste hunter. A strange correlation that I note but cannot explain.

This story, from Book Fourteen of the *Mahabharata*, is not part of the conversation between Yudhishthira and Vyasa, but is told directly by the bard Vaisampayana, on the outer layer of the text.

The Text

Vaisampayana said:

On one occasion, Krishna was pleased with Uttanka and offered him a boon. Uttanka replied, 'I would like to have water whenever I wish for it, for it is hard to get in the deserts.' And Krishna replied, 'Whenever you wish for it, think of me.' And Krishna went away.

And so, one day, Uttanka became thirsty as he wandered around in the desert; he wanted water, and he remembered Krishna. Then he saw in the desert a naked and terrifying Dalit hunter smeared with dirt and mud, surrounded by his pack of dogs, wearing a sword and a bow and a quiver of arrows. And Uttanka saw a great stream of liquid coming out of the hunter's penis. Smiling, the hunter said to him, 'Come, Uttanka, and accept this water from me. For I have taken great pity on you, seeing you so oppressed by thirst.' The sage did not accept that water, and he reviled Krishna with fierce words. Again and again the hunter said to him, 'Drink!' But Uttanka was furious, deeply agitated, and did not drink. And so, resolutely rejected by Uttanka, the hunter vanished, with his dogs.

When Uttanka saw him vanish, he felt humiliated, for he thought that Krishna had tricked him and treated him badly, as if he had not been a friend. Just then Krishna appeared on the path, and Uttanka said to him, 'It was not proper for you to give to me, a leading Brahmin, water in such a form, in the piss of a Dalit hunter.' Krishna replied to Uttanka, conciliating him with smooth words, 'I gave it to you the only way I could, but you didn't understand it. I spoke to Indra for your sake. I said, "Give Uttanka the elixir of immortality in the form of water." But Indra said to me, over and over again, "A mortal should not become immortal. Give him some other boon." Finally, when I insisted that you must be given the elixir of immortality, Indra replied, conciliating me, "If the elixir of immortality really has to be given to Uttanka, then I will become a Dalit hunter and give it to him. If Uttanka accepts the elixir today in that form, I will give it to him. But if he rejects me, I will not give it to him." This is the agreement that Indra made, and he approached you in that form and you rejected him when he offered you the elixir. The god had the form of a Chandala hunter, and you made a serious mistake. But I will do what more I can about your wish. I will make your desire for water bear fruit. On any days when a desire for water arises in you in the desert, clouds filled with water will appear and provide you with delicious water, and they will become famous as "Uttanka clouds".'

Uttanka was delighted to hear this from Krishna. And even today, 'Uttanka clouds' bring rain in the desert.

[14.54]

VII. Stories about Shiva

Shiva inherits much of the mythology of Indra, but he also generates a whole new world of his own myths.[30] Our first text in this section explicitly addresses the historical fact that Shiva is not one of the Vedic gods—and therefore is not included among the gods to whom offerings are made in Vedic sacrifices. Yet, by the time of the *Mahabharata*, Shiva had become a god, now much greater than Indra, and was the recipient of important non-Vedic sacrifices. The text expresses this shift in theological power through the metaphor of violence: Shiva, the uninvited guest at the Vedic sacrifice, breaks in and destroys it until he is finally granted a special portion of his own, still not really a part of the Vedic ritual. But in a final backward-glancing Vedic connection, Shiva is said to have created the Fever that Indra used to destroy Vritra.

The final story in our collection reflects a later moment in Shiva's history, when he is a very great god indeed, now closely assimilated to Agni, the god of fire. Shiva himself in this text is not a warrior who battles demons, but he is the father of the great general of the gods, the warrior and demon-slayer Skanda. And so the treasured Vedic myth is carried along over the centuries into the *Mahabharata*.

34. How Shiva, Excluded from Daksha's Sacrifice, Created Fever

We have already seen a story of the origin of disease in the tale of Death as a maiden, and a story of the creation of fever in the course of Indra's battle with Vritra. This version of the origin of fever begins with the Vritra story but then retells it quite differently, now attributing the victory not to Indra but to Shiva, a god of the *Mahabharata* who inherits much of the mythology of the Vedic Indra but is not, as this text rightly insists, part of the original Vedic pantheon.

The Text

Yudhishthira said, 'A question has arisen in me about the killing of Vritra. As you told the story, I gathered that Vritra was deluded by a fever and then was killed by Indra with his thunderbolt. But how and where did this fever come from? I want to hear about the origin of fever, in precise detail.' Bhishma said, 'Listen while I tell you, in full detail, about the origin of fever, as the story is well known in the world.'

Once upon a time there was a peak of Mount Meru called 'Luminous' [*jyotishka*], famous throughout the triple world. It was immeasurable; no one in all the worlds could climb it, and all the jewels there are were there on its surface. There, on a peak shining with golden ore, the god Shiva sat on a divan, honoured by all the sages and gods, and his wife Parvati stayed always at his side.

After some time, a creator god named Daksha[31] decided to perform a sacrifice. All the gods, with Indra at their head, decided to attend his sacrifice. With Shiva's permission, they went to the 'Gateway of the Ganges'[32] in their blazing chariots; so it has been heard.

But when Parvati saw that the gods were going there, she said to her husband Shiva, 'My lord, where are the gods going, led by Indra? Tell me truly, for this worries me greatly.' Shiva said, 'A great creator god named Daksha is giving a horse sacrifice, and all the inhabitants of heaven are going there.' Parvati said, 'Why aren't you going to this sacrifice? What is preventing you from going?' Shiva said, 'This is all agreed among the gods themselves: in all sacrifices, no share is designated for me. This is the path that was previously and rightly devised: in keeping with dharma, the gods do not offer me any portion of the sacrifice.'

Parvati said: 'Among all creatures, you excel in your virtues. You cannot be conquered or even assailed, because of your energy and fame and glory. This denial of your share makes me so unhappy that I tremble.' Then the goddess remained silent, but her mind was on fire. Knowing her thoughts, and what in her heart she wanted to have done, Shiva summoned his companion and vehicle, the bull Nandi, and said, 'Wait.' Activating the power of his yoga, and with the help of his terrifying followers, he suddenly attacked that sacrifice and destroyed it. Some of his followers roared, and some laughed; others sprinkled the fire with blood. Some who had grotesque faces uprooted the sacrificial stakes and whirled them around; others opened their great mouths and swallowed up the sacrificial servants.

Then, as the sacrifice was attacked on all sides, it took the form of a deer and flew up into the sky. But Shiva, realizing that the sacrifice had taken that form and had fled, took up his bow and arrow and flew after it.[33] Then, out of his anger a terrible drop of sweat appeared on his forehead. As soon as that drop of sweat fell on the ground, a tremendous fire broke out, like the fire of doomsday. And out of that fire a terrifying man was born, with very red eyes and a tawny beard. His hair stuck straight up, and his short body was very hairy, but layered like that of a hawk or an owl. His skin was dark and he had a gaping mouth; he wore red clothes. All the gods ran away in terror in all directions. He burnt up that sacrifice as a fire burns tinder, and then he began to wander about. The earth quaked, and a cry of 'Alas!' arose from the terrified people.

Then Brahma appeared before Shiva and said, 'All the gods will give you, too, a portion. Withdraw your destruction, for all these gods and sages find no respite from your anger. As for this man who was born from your sweat, let him wander through the worlds under the name of Fever. But, since the entire earth would not be able to bear his energy if it remained in one piece, let him be divided into many parts.' That is what Brahma said to Shiva. And when a portion of the sacrifice had been ordained for Shiva, he said, 'Yes,' to Brahma. Then Shiva became supremely happy and even began to smile, because he was given a share, in accordance with Brahma's promise.

Shiva divided Fever up into many parts, for the sake of all creatures. The disease of rut in the heads of elephants, the exudation of minerals in mountains, the indigo plants in the waters, and the slough of snakes; diseases in the feet of cows, saline places on the surface of the earth, and blindness in domestic animals; diseases in the indentation in the heads of horses, in the crests of peacocks, diseases of the eye in cuckoos—Shiva created all of these and proclaimed that they were all aspects of fever. And the rupture in the bile of goats; exhaustion among tigers; and hiccups[34] in all creatures, even parrots—all that is also known as fever. And something called fever, that can enter a man at the time of death, or birth, or the middle of life, is well known among humans. What we call fever is the terrible energy of Shiva.

When that fever penetrated Vritra, he yawned, and then Indra hurled his thunderbolt into him. When the thunderbolt entered Vritra, it shattered him, and when he had been shattered by the thunderbolt, the great demon, who was also a great yogi, went to the highest dwelling place of Vishnu. For, in the past, he had filled the universe with his devotion to Vishnu, and therefore when he was slain in battle, he reached Vishnu's abode. And so I have told you, in great detail, how the great fever entered Vritra.

[12.274]

35. How Shiva Swallowed Shukra

Shiva inherits much of the mythology of Indra, including a cult of Shiva's phallus (the *lingam*) distantly descended from Indra's phallic mythology (of which we have caught a glimpse in the story of Uttanka and the low-caste hunter). Shukra, the consigliere of the demons, is so named because he is born through the same phallic path through which semen (*shukra*) emerges from Shiva's body. The word *shukra* may here also carry another of its meanings: 'bright', for Shukra is also the planet Venus.

The Text

Yudhishthira said, 'I've always been curious about this and would love to know the truth about it: The divine sage Shukra always took pleasure in doing what was good for the demons and bad for the gods. Why did he always strengthen the vital power of the demons? Why was there always this enmity between the demons and the gods? How did Shukra become the consigliere of the demons? And how did he become so successful? I want to know all about this.' Bhishma replied: 'Listen attentively and I will tell you truly all that I heard before.'

Shukra did what pleased the demons, on any occasion for which he had sympathy. Kubera was king of the Yakshas and Rakshasas, and he was also in charge of the treasure of the universe. Shukra, who was a master of yoga, entered Kubera, paralysed him by yoga, and stole his wealth. Then Kubera was filled with an anger that demanded revenge; deeply disturbed, he went to Shiva and reported to him: 'Shukra paralysed me with his yoga and stole my wealth; and then he used his yoga to escape.'

When Shiva, himself a great yogi, heard this, he became angry. His eyes were red as he picked up his trident, and he said, 'Where is he? Where is he?' Shukra was far away from him, but he knew what Shiva wanted to do. He realized how angry the great yogi Shiva was, and he worried about whether he should run away, advance, or stay where he was. He used his fierce *tapas* to think about Shiva and used his yoga to imagine himself on the tip of Shiva's trident. But Shiva, an archer made adept by his *tapas*, realized what form Shukra had taken, and with his hand he bent his trident. When Shiva saw that Shukra, on the tip of the trident, had come into his hand, he opened his mouth and, with his hand, gently tossed Shukra in. Shukra went down into Shiva's stomach and wandered about there.

Yudhishthira asked, 'Why did Shukra wander around in Shiva's stomach? What did he do there?' Bhishma said:

At first, Shiva entered the waters and remained there, still as a pillar, for a million years. After engaging in this difficult *tapas*, he stood up out of the great lake, and then Brahma came to him and asked him if he was well, and if his *tapas* had gone well. Shiva replied, 'Very well, thanks.' But then, through his powers of yoga, Shiva saw that something was growing inside him. He entered a deep yoga of meditation, and Shukra, who had settled down in Shiva's stomach, became greatly disturbed. Staying right there, Shukra praised Shiva; hoping to get out, he struck back at him with his energy. From inside Shiva's stomach, Shukra said, 'Have mercy on me,' again and again. Then Shiva said to him, 'Go and free yourself through my penis.' And as he said this, Shiva obstructed all the other openings of the body. When Shukra saw that he had been shut in on all sides, he wandered about here and there, burnt by Shiva's energy. Finally, as he could find no other door, he came out through Shiva's penis, and so got the name of Shukra ['semen'].

When Shiva saw Shukra coming out, blazing with energy, he was filled with rage and took up his trident in his hand, but the goddess Parvati, Shiva's wife, restrained Shiva in his rage, and Shukra became a child of the goddess. She said to Shiva, 'You should not harm him; he has become my son. For no one who has come out of the stomach of a god deserves to be destroyed.' Then Shiva was pleased by the goddess Parvati, and laughing, he said, over and over, 'Let him go wherever he wants!' Then Shukra bowed to the god who had granted him this boon, and to the goddess too, and went where he wanted to go.

[12.278]

36. How Skanda Was Born and Taraka was Killed

An even more complicated birth story is told of a far more important son of Shiva: the god Skanda, the general of the gods, who rides, appropriately for an army officer, on a peacock. He has multiple parents, but he is often called Karttikeya because one set of his parents consists of the Pleiades (Krittikas). The story of his birth is a bit bizarre, even for a Hindu god,[35] but the closing description of the baby shower is quite humanly charming.

The Text

Bhishma said that, of all the many gifts one could give to Brahmins, gold was the best. Yudhishthira asked Bhishma to tell him about gold. Bhishma told him this story.

When the marriage of Shiva to the goddess Parvati had taken place, on the highest mountain Himalaya, all the gods became distressed and went to Shiva. Bowing their heads to Shiva and to the goddess, they all said to Shiva, 'This union of yours with the goddess is a union of a man who has *tapas* with a woman who has *tapas*, the union of a woman of fiery glory with a man who has extremely fiery glory. Your seed is never shed in vain, and this goddess is just like that too. The offspring of the two of you will be doubly powerful, and certainly nothing at all will be left in the three worlds. The gods are bowing down before you; grant them a boon. If you wish to do what is best for the three worlds, withhold your blazing seed from the making of offspring.'

'So be it,' Shiva replied to the gods. And as he said this, he drew his seed up, and from that moment on he has remained with his seed drawn up. But the goddess became furious when he had cut off her progeny, and she spoke harsh words to the gods, because of her nature as a woman: 'My husband wanted to have children, but you turned him back from that. Therefore, all of you gods will be without children. Since you cut off my fertility today, all of you gods will be infertile.' And the gods and goddesses became childless because of that curse.

But Fire was not there at the time of the curse. And, though Shiva held back his matchless seed, a very little bit of it spilled from him and fell there on the earth. Then it fell into the fire and grew large in a marvellous way.

Now, at this very time, the gods, headed by Indra, were badly tormented by a demon named Taraka, whose aggression terrified them. The demon stole the gods' homes and their celestial chariots and cities and the sages' ashrams. The minds of all the gods and sages were distressed, and they sought refuge with Brahma. They said: 'You gave the demon Taraka a boon, that he could not be killed by any of the gods, and now he is oppressing the gods and sages. Devise a way for him to be killed. We are terrified of him. Save us! We have no other refuge.' Brahma said, 'I am impartial to all creatures, but the violation of dharma in this instance does not please me. Let Taraka be killed right away, for he is oppressing the gods and sages. The Vedas and dharma must not be destroyed. I already arranged this in the past. Do not be distressed.' The gods said, 'The demon is proud of his power because of the boon you gave him. He cannot be killed by the gods, so how can he be subdued? For you gave him the boon that he could not be killed by any of the gods or demons or Rakshasas, and Shiva cursed the gods: "You will have no offspring!"'

Brahma said: 'Fire was not there at the time of the curse. Let him produce a son to slaughter those who hate the gods, a son surpassing all the gods and demons and Rakshasas and men and Gandharvas and snakes and birds. With his spear, a weapon that never falls in vain, this son will kill the one who has frightened you and he will kill all the other enemies of the gods. For the marvellous fiery seed that Shiva shed into the fire will be born in the Ganges to destroy the enemies of the gods. Since Fire did not receive the curse, as he was absent, the son of Shiva will be born through him to remove your fears. Search for Fire today and urge him to do this. I have told you the way to kill Taraka. For those who have *tapas* may slay even those who have been granted boons that make them invincible.

'Desire is the most enduring fire, the lord of the universe, impossible to predict; he goes everywhere and creates everything. He lies in the heart of all creatures and is even older than Shiva. Search for Fire quickly, for he is a great mass of fiery energy. He is the god who will bring about what you long for in your hearts.'

When the gods heard this, they felt that their wishes had been granted, and they went in search of Fire. All the sages joined the gods and searched the three worlds, hoping for a sight of Fire, thinking of nothing but him. Armed with supreme *tapas*, they searched all the worlds. But Fire had disappeared into the waters, and so they did not find him. They began to worry, and their hearts were weary, but they still longed eagerly for a sight of Fire.

Then a frog that lived in the water and had been burnt by Fire's energy rose up out of the surface of the water and said to the gods, 'Fire is living in the watery depths. I came here because of the heat that came from Fire. As Fire was sleeping in the water, he heated the water with his flames, and that was what heated us. If you gods wish to see Fire, or if you need Fire to do something for you, go to him there. We will have accomplished our purpose. But, because of our fear of Fire, we will go now.'

And when the frog had said this much, he quickly entered the water. But Fire found out that the frog had carried this tale against him, and he cursed him: 'You will not know any tastes.' Then Fire went away to live somewhere else, and he did not reveal himself to the gods.

But the gods did a favour for the frogs; listen and I will tell you all about it.

The gods said, 'Because of Fire's curse you will have no tongue and will never know tastes. But you will voice many forms of speech. You will live in holes without food and without thought. But even when you have no life's breath in you and are all dried out, the earth will sustain you. And you will move about in the night even when it is entirely dark.' And the waters in the underground level that Fire had passed through, that had been heated up by the energy of Fire when he lay down in them, released their heat through mountain streams.

Then the gods once again wandered around this earth, searching for Fire, but still they did not find him. An elephant said to the gods, 'Fire is in a fig tree.' Fire, swooning with rage, cursed all the elephants: 'Your tongue will bend back.' Since the elephant had pointed him out, Fire came out of the fig tree and entered the hollow of a hardwood tree,[36] because he wanted to sleep. But the gods, pleased by the elephants' steadfast dedication to the truth, did a favour for them. The gods said: 'Even with your tongue bent back, you will be able to eat all foods. And you will utter loud speech, though with indistinct syllables.' And then the gods once again went to find Fire.

Fire had left the fig tree and was now inside the hardwood tree. A parrot told the gods where he was, and they ran to find him there. Fire cursed the parrot: 'You will be without speech.' And Fire turned back the parrot's tongue. But when the gods saw Fire, they were filled with pity for the parrot and they said, 'Your speech will not be entirely destroyed, parrot. Your tongue will be turned back but your speech will be lovely, indistinct but marvellous and melodious, like the speech of a child or an old man.' And ever since then, fire is found inside hardwood trees, and men have made that wood the means of kindling fire.

Then the gods saw Fire inside the hardwood tree, and they made it a holy place for sacred fire, in all rituals. When Fire saw the gods, he became worried and asked them, 'Why have you come?' The gods and the supreme sages said to him, 'We must engage you in a task that you ought to do.' Fire said, 'Tell me what you want to have done, and I will do it all. For you must use me. You must not hesitate about this.' The gods said, 'A demon named Taraka was given a boon by Brahma and now has such power that he harasses us. He must be killed. Protect the bands of gods and sages. Beget a child full of energy, who will put an end to our fear of the demon. We have been cursed by the goddess and so have no other refuge but your seed. Therefore, protect us!'

Fire said, 'Yes!' and went to the heavenly Ganges. He mingled with her and created in her an embryo that grew in her womb just as fire grows in kindling wood. But the Ganges swooned because of the energy of that embryo; she experienced such sharp pain that she was unable to bear it. Then the demon Taraka uttered a great roar, terrifying the Ganges, whose eyes dimmed and rolled about as she lost consciousness, for she was not able to bear that embryo by herself. Trembling, oppressed by the power of the embryo, her limbs overcome by its energy, the Ganges said, 'I cannot bear this energy. It stupefies me, makes me ill and confused. I must give it up, however unwillingly, because of my pain and misery. No agreement was ever made between my mind and that of Fire; this union took place because of a disaster.'

Then Fire said to her, 'He must be borne, must be born. This embryo filled with my energy will give rise to great virtues and good results. There is nothing that you cannot attain by holding on to my seed.' But though Fire and the gods tried to stop her, the Ganges released that embryo. She was so harassed and violated by Shiva's energy that she did not have the physical strength to hold on to the embryo. Driven by her pain and misery as the embryo blazed like a fire, she released it on Mount Meru.

Then Fire saw the Ganges and asked her, 'Is the infant doing well? What sort of complexion does he have, and what sort of body? And what energy? Tell me all of this!' The Ganges said, 'The infant is golden, with energy like yours. Golden, spotless, blazing, lighting up the mountain. His perfume is like that of Kadamba flowers, as cool as lakes covered with lotus leaves. Anything on the earth or in the mountains that is touched by the energy of this infant, as if by the rays of the sun, all of that shines like gold all around. He runs around the mountains and the rivers and the streams, illuminating the triple world, moving and still, with his energy. That is what your son looks like, Fire. Like the sun in its beauty, or like another moon.' When the goddess Ganges had said this, she vanished. And so Fire, having accomplished with his energy what had to be done for the gods, went to his own favourite place. It is because of these deeds and qualities that the sages and gods call Fire 'Golden Seed'.

Yudhishthira said, 'Tell me how Taraka was destroyed. You have said that he could not be killed by the gods, but you have not described his death in detail here. I want to hear this from you in its entirety; I have a great curiosity about the death of Taraka.' Bhishma said:

That infant of great energy, begotten by Fire in the Ganges, came to a divine grove of reeds, and there he grew and took on a marvellous appearance. The Pleiades saw him, shining like the young sun, and immediately affection arose in them for the child. The deities and sages, in great distress, had urged the Pleiades to nurse the child. For no single female among the deities was able to nurse the child of Fire, because of his great power and energy. But Fire was pleased that all six Pleiades would nurse the infant born from his own energy and his supreme seed. So the child divided himself into six, and the six Pleiades nurtured the six-fold infant of Fire and nourished him with the milk from their breasts, and the entire energy of fire was placed in the six Pleiades. But as their limbs were overcome by the energy of Skanda as he grew, when the time arrived, the Pleiades gave up the six infants, who united as one child with six heads.

And so he was called Kumara ['the Youth'], and Karttikeya [from the Krittikas, the Pleiades], and Skanda [because the seed had been emitted, *skanna*], and Guha [because he had lived in secret, *guha*]. All the gods went there to see the son of Fire. The sages praised him and the Gandharvas sang to him. He had six faces and twelve eyes, twelve arms, and a fleshy chest, and he shone like fire and the sun. He loved Brahmins. When the gods and sages saw him lying in the thicket of reeds, they rejoiced, because they regarded the demon Taraka as as good as killed.

Then all the gods set out to please him, and as he was playing, they gave him things to play with, and whole flocks of birds. Garuda gave him a peacock with brightly coloured feathers, and the Rakshasas gave him a boar and a buffalo. Varuna gave him a rooster that blazed like fire, and the Moon gave him a ram; the Sun gave him a shining light. The goddess who is the mother cow, Surabhi, gave him hundreds of thousands of cows; and

Fire gave him an excellent goat. Ila gave him a lot of flowers and fruit. Tvashtri gave him a cart and a chariot. Varuna gave him tame serpents and divine fish. Indra gave him lions and tigers and elephants and other animals with teeth. And the bands of Rakshasas and demons who followed Shiva gave him many terrible beasts of prey and all sorts of umbrellas.

As the demon Taraka saw the god growing up, he tried to kill him in various ways, but he was not able to do it. The gods honoured Skanda and made him their general; and they told him the unpleasant things that Taraka had done. The powerful god, general of the gods, grew up and was very strong. He killed the demon Taraka with his irresistible spear. And when Skanda, the mighty general, the protector of the gods, had killed the demon, Indra was once again established as the king of the gods. Then Skanda went back to just playing, doing what pleased Shiva.

[13.83]

Glossary of Names and Sanskrit Terms

Adharma, the absence or violation of dharma
Agastya, a great sage
Agni, Fire, god of fire
Ahalya, an adulterous woman, the wife of the sage Gautama, seduced by Indra
Anushasana, instruction, name of the thirteenth book of the *Mahabharata*
Apsaras, a celestial courtesan and dancing girl, partner of a Gandharva
Arjuna Kartavirya, a powerful and destructive Kshatriya
artha, political and material success, the second of the three aims of life
Arthashastra, the Machiavellian political textbook attributed to Brihaspati
Arundhati, virtuous wife of the sage Vasishtha
ashram, a hermitage
Ashtavakra, 'Crooked in Eight Ways', a Brahmin sage
Asuras, celestial demons, the enemies of the gods
atman, the self, the immortal spirit inside each person
Atri, one of the Seven Sages
Avikampaka, a king who mourns for his son
Bhangashvana, a royal sage who became a woman
Bharadvaja, one of the Seven Sages
Bhishma, the old king
Brahma, the creator god
Brahmin, priest, the highest of the four Hindu classes
Brihaspati, the consigliere of the gods; mythical author of the *Arthashastra*

Chandala, an outcaste or Dalit hunter

charu, a consecrated pudding of milk and rice, given to a woman to make her pregnant with a son

Dadhicha, a Vedic sage

Daksha, a creator god, whose several daughters were married to several gods

Devasharman, a sage, husband of Ruchi

Dharma, religion, morality

Durvasas, a short-tempered sage whose name means 'Badly housed' or 'Bad to house'

Duryodhana, cousin and enemy of Yudhishthira

Gadhi, a sage, father of Satyavati

Gandharva, a celestial musician, partner of an Apsaras

Ganges, a great river that flows in heaven (the Milky Way) and on earth

gati (literally, 'going'), a person's final resting place, or final destination, the ultimate condition that one's karma will bring one to, in heaven or hell or a rebirth on earth

Gautama, a sage, husband of Ahalya; also the name of an ungrateful Brahmin; and the name of one of the Seven Sages

Ghritachi ('Shining with butter'), an Apsaras, mother of Shuka

Indra, king of the gods, god of rain and thunder

Jamadagni, son of Richika and Satyavati, father of Parashu Rama, husband of Renuka; one of the Seven Sages

Janamejaya, a king, descendant of the Pandavas, to whom the *Mahabharata* is narrated

Kala, time, also fate

Kalakavrikshaya, a sage with a crow

Kali Yuga, the last and worst of the four Ages

kama, desire, the third of the three human goals

karma, action; more particularly, the cumulative actions that determine a person's subsequent life and rebirth

Kashyapa, a great ancient sage, father of many daughters and many sons among both gods and demons; one of the Seven Sages

Krishna, an incarnation of Vishnu, husband of Rukmini, father of Pradyumna

Krita Yuga, the first of the four Ages, the Golden Age
Krittikas, the Pleiades, step-mothers of Skanda
Kshatriya, royal warrior, the second of the four Hindu classes
Kshemadarshin, King of the Kosalas
Kubera, god of the Yakshas and Rakshasas and guardian of the treasure of the gods
Kurukshetra, a sacred plain in the centre of India
kusha, a sacred grass used in sacrifices, also sharp enough to be used as a knife
Kushika, a king, father of the sage Gadhi
Madayanti, wife of the cannibal king Soudasa
Markandeya, an ancient sage
Matanga, an outcaste hunter
moksha, freedom from rebirth
Nagas, magical cobras who live in the watery world under the earth
Nandi, the bull on which Shiva rides
Nahusha, an ancient king who usurped Indra's throne
Narada, a wandering sage, carrier of tales, who often gets into mischief himself
Nishadas, outcaste tribal people
Oghavati, a princess, wife of Sudarshana the son of Fire
Panchachuda, an Apsaras
Parashu Rama, 'Rama with an Axe', son of Vishvamitra, who kills off all the Kshatriyas and also kills his mother, at his father's command
Parvan, a 'section', a book of the *Mahabharata*
Parvata, a nephew of Narada
Parvati, 'Daughter of the mountain', wife of Shiva
Pradyumna, son of Krishna and Rukmini
Prithu, the first king
Rajadharma, king of the herons
raksh, to control, protect, and guard
Rakshasa, an earth-bound demon or goblin
Renuka, wife of Jamadagni
Richika, a Brahmin sage, father of Jamadagni and Vishvamitra

Ruchi, wife of the sage Devasharman
Rukmini, wife of Krishna, mother of Pradyumna
Satyavati, daughter of Gadhi, wife of Richika, mother of Jamadagni
Seven Sages, a famous group of holy Brahmins
Shachi ('Power'), the wife of Indra
Shaibya, a wicked king
Shanti, peace, name of the twelfth book of the *Mahabharata*
sharabha, a fabulous and very dangerous beast—more dangerous than a lion or an elephant—with eight legs, four of them on top of his body
Shudra, servant, the lowest of the four Hindu classes
Shuka, 'parrot', a son of Vyasa
Shukra, consigliere of the demons, also called Ushanas
Shunahshakha ('Friend of a Dog'), Indra in disguise
Shvapaka ('Dog-cooker'), a term of abuse in early Sanskrit texts used to refer to a Dalit caste
Skanda, a son of Shiva, born of Fire, general of the gods
Soma, a plant whose intoxicating juice was offered to the gods at the Vedic sacrifice; also the name of the god who is the incarnation of the plant
Soudasa, a king cursed to become a man-eating Rakshasa
Srinjaya, a king, father of a daughter, Sukumari ('Lovely Maiden'), and a son, Suvarnashtivin ('Gold-excreting')
Sudarshana, son of Fire and the daughter of King Duryodhana
Sukumari ('Lovely Maiden'), daughter of king Srinjaya
Suprabha, daughter of the sage Vadanya and wife of the sage Ashtavakra
Surabhi, a divine cow that lives in heaven
Suvarnashtivin ('Gold-excreting'), son of king Srinjaya
tapas, ascetic heat
Taraka, a great demon killed by Skanda
Tvashtri, the artisan of the gods, father of Vishvarupa
Uma, a name of Parvati, the wife of Shiva
Upashruti, 'the Listener', a supernatural voice
Ushanas, the consigliere of the demons, also called Shukra
Utathya, a Brahmin who marries the daughter of Soma

Uttanka, disciple of the sage Gautama
Vadanya, a sage, father of Suprabha
Vaishya, merchant or farmer, the third of the four Hindu classes
Varuna, god of the waters
Vasishtha, a Brahmin sage, one of the Seven Sages
Vena, a wicked king, father of Prithu the good king
Vidura, a sage with magical powers
Vipula, a sage, disciple of Devasharman
Virajas, 'Passionless', an ancestor of Prithu
Virupaksha, a king of the Rakshasas
Vishvamitra, a great sage, son of Gadhi and of Satyavati's mother; father of Parashu Rama, a Kshatriya who becomes a Brahmin; one of the Seven Sages
Vishvarupa ('Taking All Forms'), a great demon killed by Indra
Vritra, a demon and serpent, killed by Indra
Vyasa, a great sage, author of the *Mahabharata*, grandfather of Yudhishthira, father of Shuka
Yaksha, a forest spirit
Yama, god of the dead
Yatudhani ('Womb of Demons'), a witch employed by King Shaibya
yoga, a mental and physical praxis of controlling the senses and the mind, often producing supernatural powers
Yudhishthira, the reigning king
Yuga, an Age of time; there are four: Krita is the first, and the Kali Yuga the last

Endnotes

1 Bhishma finally dies at the end of the thirteenth book, but a few moral and mythological stories, told by other narrators, are also incorporated into the fourteenth book, and I have included three of them here. Krishna also narrates some of the stories to Yudhishthira.

2 I translated these final books under the title of *After the War: The Last Books of the Mahabharata* (New Delhi: Speaking Tiger, and New York: Oxford University Press, 2022).

3 The punishment of being eaten by dogs is also what the Hebrew Bible prescribed for Jezebel (2 Kings 9.36).

4 Manu 9.11–18. In *The Laws of Manu*, a new translation of the *Manavadharmasastra* by Wendy Doniger with Brian K. Smith (Harmondsworth: Penguin Classics, 1991).

5 The submarine mare is a Hindu mythological image signifying the pent-up fires of doomsday, ready to burst out at any moment. Significantly, it is a mare, a *female* horse, that holds this fire under the ocean. See Wendy Doniger, *Winged Stallions and Wicked Mares: Horses in Indian Myth and History* (Charlottesville and London: University of Virginia Press, and New Delhi: Speaking Tiger, 2021).

6 I am using 'demons' to translate Asuras, literally 'non-gods', the celestial enemies of the gods. Brihaspati is regarded as the divine author of the cynical and devious political textbook, the *Arthashastra* that we have, and his opposite number, Shukra, is

here presumed to have composed a competing text for the demons, a text lost to us.

7 Doniger, *After the War*, p. 108.

8 *Ramayana* 7.30.17–36.

9 See also Wendy Doniger, *Splitting the Difference: Gender and Myth in Ancient Greece and India* (Chicago: University of Chicago Press, 1999), pp. 88–132.

10 *Bhagavadajjuka-Prahasanam* of Bodhayana (ed. Prabhata Sastri) (Prayaga: Devabhasaprakasanam, 1979), verse 32.

11 The final resting place, or final destination, called the *gati* (literally, the 'going'), is the ultimate condition that each person's karma will bring that person to, in heaven or hell or a rebirth on earth.

12 The fig tree is the *udumbara* and the banyan is the *ashvattha*.

13 *Brahmapurana* 212.83–85. Wendy Doniger O'Flaherty (ed.), *Textual Sources for the Study of Hinduism* (Chicago: University of Chicago Press, 1990).

14 Recall the allusion to Indra's punishment for the seduction of Gautama's wife, Ahalya, in the story of Vipula and Ruchi, above.

15 This conflict did not particularly bother Parashu Rama when he found himself in a similar quandary, for he obeyed the command of his father (Jamadagni) when he ordered him to behead his mother, Renuka, for what the father wrongly perceived as her sexual peccadillo, in a famous story that we will not consider here. See *Kathasaritsagara* 12.130 and Wendy Doniger, *Splitting the Difference: Gender and Myth in Ancient Greece and India*, pp. 204–32.

16 Presumably Ahalya's adultery.

17 Recall 'How Satyavati's Mother Corrupted Her Daughter's Pregnancy'.

18 See Doniger, *After the War*.

19 See above, pp. 19–21.

20 See story #7 above (pp. 69–73).

21 'How the Fish with Presence of Mind and the Farsighted Fish Survived, and the Dilatory Fish Died'; 'How the Rat Escaped from the Cat, the Owl, the Mongoose, and the Hunter'.

22 He is descended from Kashyapa, as the Rakshasas are.

23 See Wendy Doniger O'Flaherty, *The Origins of Evil in Hindu Mythology* (Berkeley: University of California, 1976).

24 *Na-pumsaka*, often translated as 'hermaphrodite', but actually a third gender.

25 Robert Frost, 'Nothing Gold Can Stay'.

26 This rhetoric is much like that of Shylock's speech in *The Merchant of Venice* (Act 3, Scene 1): 'Hath not a Jew eyes? Hath not a Jew hands, organs, dimensions, senses, affections, passions? Fed with the same food, hurt with the same weapons, subject to the same diseases, healed by the same means, warmed and cooled by the same winter and summer, as a Christian is?'

27 It seems odd that Shukra, rather than Brihaspati, should have been the first king's consigliere, but that's what the text says, perhaps concealing an ironic moral.

28 A supernatural voice.

29 In another text that we have considered ('How Indra Killed Vritra and Suffered from Brahminicide'), the division was between Apsarases, fire, grasses and water.

30 See Wendy Doniger O'Flaherty, *Asceticism and Eroticism in the Mythology of Siva* (Oxford University Press, 1973; retitled *Siva: The Erotic Ascetic*, 1981).

31 Daksha ('dexterous') was the father of many goddesses who married the ancient gods. In some tellings of this story, Daksha is the father of Shiva's wife, but not, apparently, in this version. See Doniger O'Flaherty, *Siva: The Erotic Ascetic*.

32 Gangadvara, 'Gateway of the Ganges', is the place where the river Ganges flows from the Himalayas into the Indo-Gangetic plain.

33 The deer eventually becomes a constellation called Mrigashiras, 'Deer's Head', which we call Orion, the Hunter.

34 Sanskrit: *hikkika*.

35 See Doniger O'Flaherty, *Siva: The Erotic Ascetic*.

36 The tree from which firesticks are made; the wood used to kindle fires.